SURVEY OF LONDON

GENERAL EDITOR: JOHN GREENACOMBE

Docklands in the Making: The Redevelopment of The Isle of Dogs, 1981–1995

Alan Cox

THE ATHLONE PRESS
Published for the Royal Commission on the
Historical Monuments of England
1995

First published 1995 by
THE ATHLONE PRESS
1, Park Drive, London NW11 7SG
and 165 First Avenue, Atlantic Highlands, NJ 07716
for the
ROYAL COMMISSION ON THE HISTORICAL MONUMENTS OF ENGLAND

British Library Cataloguing in Publication Data
A catalogue record for this book is available from the British Library

ISBN 0 485 48500 1

Library of Congress Cataloging-in-Publication Data
Cataloging in Publication data applied for

The publication of this book has been assisted by a
grant from the London Docklands Development
Corporation

Printed and bound in Great Britain by Balding + Mansell, Peterborough and London

Chairman's Preface

As the body responsible for maintaining and enhancing the National Monuments Record, the Royal Commission has a duty not only to record historic buildings and sites, but also to make a record of new buildings before time and our English climate have robbed them of their bloom. Nowhere in the country has the construction of striking new buildings been greater than in London's Docklands, which have been transformed over the last fifteen years and now boast one of the largest concentrations of late-twentieth-century architecture and architectural styles to be seen anywhere in the world. The Commission recorded many of these buildings for the Survey of London's two volumes on *Poplar, Blackwall and The Isle of Dogs*, published in 1994. Continuing interest in the development of Docklands has now prompted the Commission to re-issue the Survey's study of the new Docklands buildings in a compact form. The original text has been re-organized, and, such is the pace of redevelopment, several new buildings have been included which were not in existence when the Survey went to press only last year. The illustrations, too, have been revised and expanded, the majority of the photographs being the Commission's own. Copies of these photographs are held in the NMR's London search room at 55 Blandford Street.

The text of this study was written and revised by Alan Cox, with contributions from Peter Guillery, Stephen Porter, Ann Robey and Philip Temple. The drawings were prepared by Michael Clements, and the photographs taken by Derek Kendall. Tara Draper compiled the index. The book was edited by Stephen Porter and designed by Wolfgang Klär, and the cover was designed by Ian Mackenzie-Kerr.

The London Docklands Development Corporation has very kindly contributed to the cost of publication, and on behalf of the Royal Commission I would like to the thank the Corporation and its Chairman, Michael Pickard, for their generous support.

FARINGDON

Commissioners

Acknowledgements

Among the many individuals and institutions who have provided invaluable help in the preparation of this book, particular thanks are due to Andrew Dick and other staff of the London Docklands Development Corporation; Bob Aspinall and Alex Werner of the Museum of London's Museum in Docklands Project; Christopher Lloyd, Harry Watton, Jerome Farrell and other staff of the Tower Hamlets Local History Library, Bancroft Road; the staff of the Greater London Record Office and History Library; the staff of the Guildhall Library; the library of the Chartered Institute of Bankers; David Bernstein of Levitt Bernstein Associates; David Mann and Lorraine Shears of the East London Housing Association; Jeremy Dixon; Keith G. Preston; Robert Thorne; Stanley Trevor; the Worshipful Company of Ironmongers; Essex Self-Build Advisory Service; Hutchinson Partners; Institution of Civil Engineers Library; John Laing Construction Ltd; London Borough of Tower Hamlets; Newman Levinson & Partners; McDonald's Restaurants Ltd; Olympia & York; Queen Mary and Westfield College; Skidmore, Owings & Merrill Inc.; Whittam Cox Ellis Clayton Partnership; Wimpey; Yorke Rosenberg & Mardall.

Contents

List of Illustrations

Except where indicated all the photographs were taken by Derek Kendall and are copyright of the RCHME. Their negative numbers are given in brackets.

List of abbreviations used on the plans

BR	bedroom	K	kitchen	Sh	shower
DR	dining room	L	lift		
G	garage	LR	living room		

CHAPTER I

The Isle of Dogs before Docklands

Cesar Pelli's skyscraper at Canary Wharf has come to symbolize not only the regeneration of London's Docklands but also the wider development boom of the late 1980s. This is hardly surprising, for the changes produced on the site of the West India Docks within just a few years were dramatic indeed. Yet the Canary Wharf Tower is only the largest and most prominent of a generation of commercial buildings and housing, in a variety of styles, loosely designated as 'Docklands'. The planning, architectural, constructional and financial aspects of the redevelopment inevitably attracted a great deal of comment, arousing more interest in the Isle of Dogs than at any time since the opening of the West India Docks in 1802. Then, as now, it was the 'stupendous scale' of the undertakings which caught the imagination of contemporaries.[1]

The low-lying and largely unpopulated peninsula of the Isle of Dogs has attracted the attention of schemers and would-be entrepreneurs over a long period, their large-scale projects ranging in viability from the hopelessly Utopian to the hard-headedly commercial. The earliest of these projects, published in 1681 by the engineer, agriculturalist and 'improver' Andrew Yarranton, was a scheme for turning much of the Island into a 'fishing city', to provide safe berths for a shipping fleet and houses for fishermen.[2] His plan, devised as a means of countering Dutch competition in the fishing industry, and more political than practical, proposed the construction of two parallel docks and a connecting channel, controlled by locks, with houses lining the quays (1). He envisaged that ancillary businesses, including the making of rope and nets, would also be established. Registration of boats and houses would help facilitate credit, and incentives, such as tax breaks and naturalization of immigrants living there, were proposed to ensure the city's success.

A century after Yarranton produced his scheme, attention was again focused on the Isle of Dogs when the construction of enclosed wet docks dedicated to the West India trade was being considered in the 1790s. It seemed to offer an ideal location, for not only was it still largely undeveloped pasture close to the City, but because of its shape the docks could be given entrances to both east and west. Yet the site was chosen only after a long debate, which generated several schemes and a strong movement in favour of building the docks at Wapping. Once the Isle of Dogs was selected, construction, which began in 1800, proceeded apace and the docks were completed in 1806.

Simultaneously, the Corporation of London bought a strip of land along the southern side of the West India

Dock Company's ground and constructed a canal there, parallel to the two dock basins. Planned as a profit-making scheme for the Corporation, this was intended to provide an attractive short cut for shipping, cutting out the tedious journey around the Island, which many travellers avoided by disembarking at Blackwall and making their way into the City along Poplar High Street and through Limehouse. In spite of this benefit, the canal failed to attract traffic and was sold to the dock company in 1829 for the surprisingly large sum of £120,000. It was subsequently converted as the South Dock of the West India system.

When the West India Docks were built development on the Isle of Dogs was confined to yards along the river front on both the west, Limehouse, side and the east side, in Coldharbour, with comparatively little housing. The yards consisted chiefly of the premises of shipbuilders, barge-builders, boat-builders, ropemakers, sailmakers and others engaged in shipping-related enterprises. None of these approached the scale of Blackwall Yard, to the north-east, which had been established by the East India Company in 1614 and sold by them in the 1650s. This was a major yard, for both the building and repairing of ships, and for much of its life was also a very profitable one. In 1789–90 the Brunswick Dock was built to supplement the existing docks in the yard. Covering eight acres, it was exceeded in size on the Thames only by the late-seventeenth-century Greenland Dock at Rotherhithe. On its western quay was a great mast-house, rising to 120ft, which for many years dominated and symbolized the area in much the same way as Canary Wharf Tower both dominates and symbolizes modern Docklands. Following the precedent of the West India merchants, those in the East India trade decided that docks dedicated to their business were preferable to continued use of river wharves. They therefore established the East India Dock Company, which acquired a part of Blackwall Yard, adapted the Brunswick Dock and added a second, larger, basin to the north. Begun in 1803, the East India Docks were opened in 1806.

In addition to these successful schemes, other, no less grandiose proposals for docks on the Isle of Dogs were produced during the early nineteenth century to provide wharfing for colliers. The first such proposal, made in 1812 and based upon the conversion of the City Canal, was defeated, largely because of opposition from the Corporation.[3] Congestion in the river was a growing problem, however, with the annual number of colliers rising from 3,452 in 1794 to 7,117 in 1824. In 1824–5 five

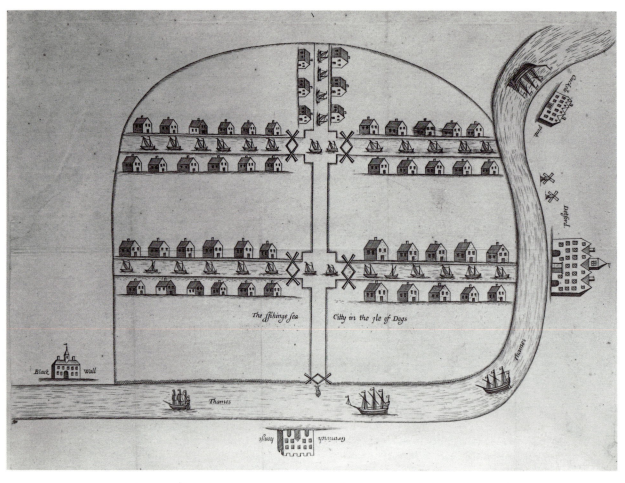

1. 'Fishing City': Andrew Yarranton's plan for the development of the Isle of Dogs, 1681.

competing schemes – eventually reduced to one – were put forward for collier docks on the Isle of Dogs. Prepared by a consortium of owners and tenants, the winning plan, by George Rennie, envisaged the creation of the largest dock system in London, extending across the northern half of the Island, south of the City Canal (*2*). There were to be two parallel rectangular docks, linked to the canal and lined with warehouses, flanked to east and west by basins and river entrances. Space was to be provided not only for the coal trade, but also for some timber and other foreign trade, gleaned from the business of the West India and East India dock companies, whose monopolies expired in 1823 and 1827 respectively.[4] The Collier Dock Company failed to raise the capital required, however, and collapsed in 1827. The next scheme, drawn up in 1836 and revised in 1837–8, eschewed excavated docks. Its designer, the architect T. Marsh Nelson, preferred instead a collier wharf, over a mile long, on an embankment along the south-east side of the Isle of Dogs (*3*).[5] This plan included a road across the Island from east to west, linked by steam-ferries to the south bank at Deptford and Greenwich Marshes, and, in its more developed form, a railway from the collier wharf connecting with the London and Blackwall Railway at Limehouse.

The need for collier docks was eventually satisfied with the opening in 1851 of Poplar Dock, to the north of the Blackwall Basin of the West India Docks. The dock company had first developed the site as reservoirs. These were converted to a timber pond in 1844 and then, in 1850–1, into a railway dock for coal and export traffic (the first of London's docks to have rail connections). It was extended to the west in 1875–7 by the addition of another basin.

With the failure of the earlier schemes, the central part of the Island south of the West India Docks remained undeveloped grazing land, a temptation to the ambitious speculator. In the late 1850s Nathaniel John Fenner, a Millwall oil merchant, and Robert Fairlie, a civil engineer, succumbed to the temptation and drew up plans for a system of enclosed wet docks there. They were unable to proceed with the scheme without assistance and so employed an agent, the engineer William Wilson, to promote it. Wilson, perhaps judging that their means were inadequate to the task, came to terms with a partnership of leading public-works contractors, John Kelk and John Aird & Son, and so it was they, not Fenner and Fairlie, who constructed the Millwall Docks in the mid-1860s. The docks were a speculation, intended not for shipping,

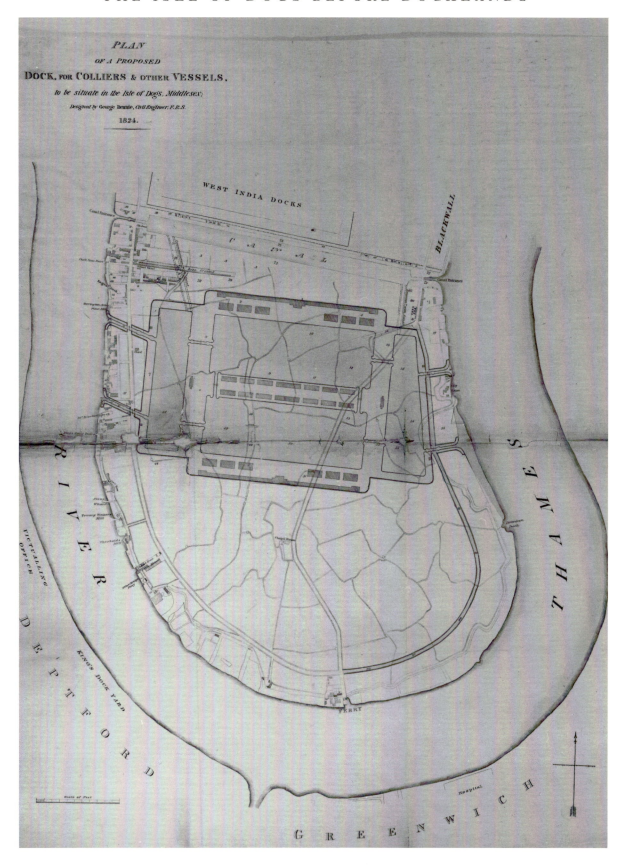

2. George Rennie's plan for a collier dock on the Isle of Dogs, 1824.

for there was already over-capacity in the port, but to provide wharfage for factories during what was then a boom period for the Island's riverside industries. The boom had come to an end by the time that the docks were opened in 1868, however, and the factories did not materialize. Indeed, the docks were never completed as intended, lacking the eastern arm of the inverted T-shape of the original design. The Millwall Dock Company, as it became in 1870, succeeded instead in attracting much commodity trade from elsewhere in the London dock system, providing a miscellany of sheds and warehouses for storage. Wool, timber and, particularly, grain were handled, and by 1900 about a third of London's grain imports and a tenth of its river-borne timber trade came through the Millwall Docks.

The last of the nineteenth-century suggestions was a dramatic scheme devised in the 1870s by Philip Revell for turning the whole of the Isle of Dogs into a fortress for the defence of London.[6] This involved shortening the course of the Thames by incorporating the import and export basins of the West India Docks into a broad new channel across the north of the Island (4). Revell believed

this would increase the flow of the river, thus carrying the river-borne sewage further out to sea and clearing the mud banks downstream from Blackwall. The abandoned meander loop would be turned into an enormous wet dock – 'the finest Dock in the world' – providing a secure anchorage for the fleet in wartime. The Island itself was to be fortified by the construction of two star-shaped forts. In Revell's view his fortress would serve to protect London as Kronstadt did St Petersburg. The many engineering difficulties exposed by the scheme did not have to be tackled because, needless to say, it never left the drawing-board.

In marked contrast to these large-scale, but coherent developments was the haphazard and piecemeal growth of the riverside industries. Indeed, the coming of the docks in the early nineteenth century seems to have had relatively little impact on the nature of the local industries, which developed independently. In addition to the growing number of shipyards and their associated trades, heavy industry was gradually established along the river during the nineteenth century, with the construction of iron works and engineering and chemical factories.

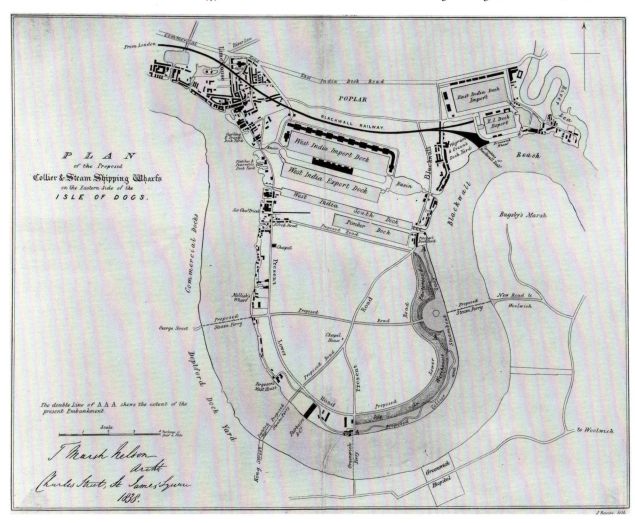

3. T. Marsh Nelson's plan for collier and steam shipping wharves on the Isle of Dogs, 1838.

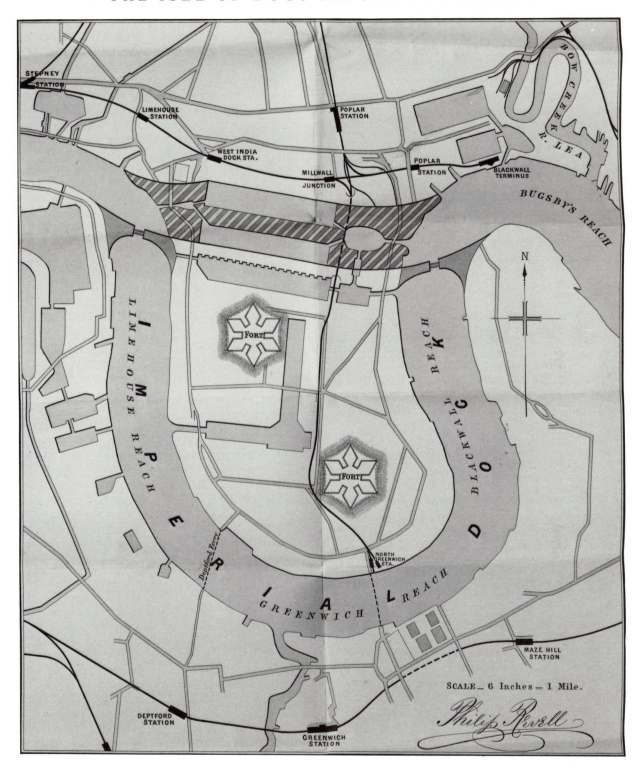

4. Philip Revell's plan for the canalization of the Thames and the defence of London, 1870s.

Nevertheless, it was iron-ship building that brought the area to public attention, particularly with the construction of the *Great Eastern* at Millwall between 1854 and 1859. Shipbuilding expanded during a period of exceptional financial and technological confidence in the 1850s and early 1860s, but the boom was short-lived and came to a crashing end following the failure of Overend Gurney & Company, bankers and money dealers, in 1866. The slump that followed was particularly severe, many of the shipyards were closed and hundreds of houses stood empty. Nevertheless, the area's industrial base was much broader than shipbuilding and its associated or dependent trades, enabling the local economy to recover during the late nineteenth century, with the population of the Island peaking around the turn of the century.

The outlines of the industrial and commercial pattern which had emerged by the mid-nineteenth century remained more or less intact until after the Second World

War, although shipbuilding declined steadily after the slump of the late 1860s. Some yards were able to continue in business until the early twentieth century by taking specialized work, and the industry experienced a brief revival during the First World War, but most of the shipbuilding capacity on the Thames was lost to the Clyde, where costs were lower. There was also a shift away from engineering, as other, lighter, manufacturing trades and the chemical industry, which was already well established, became more prominent. Even so, iron-and-steel firms such as Shaws, Westwoods, Brown Lenox and Richard Thomas & Baldwins remained major local employers until well after the Second World War. As the industrial companies failed or moved away, their premises were increasingly taken by wharfingers; wharfage, especially its shabbier and messier branches, became characteristic of the area.

By the twentieth century the docks had also undergone

5. West India Docks: aerial view looking west in 1986.

considerable change. Both the West India and East India companies had experienced changing fortunes following their most prosperous period in the early decades of the nineteenth century, before their monopolies expired. Their merger was an obvious step, effected in 1838. Among the difficulties which the joint company faced were fluctuations in trade and competition from other docks. A major worry as it struggled to diversify its trade was the inadequacy of the entrance locks, built for the sailing vessels of the early nineteenth century, to deal with the ever-larger iron ships of the Victorian era. Attempts to solve this problem at the East India Docks involved the building of a new entrance lock to the Dock Basin in 1875–9 and a new cut between the Basin and the Export Dock in 1897. At the West India Docks the works were more extensive. The South Dock was extended, with the addition of a timber pond, in 1832–3 and rebuilt and enlarged in the late 1860s, when the east entrance lock was reconstructed.

The 1870s was a prosperous decade for the docks, but this was soon reversed. The East and West India Dock Company sought to revive its declining profitability by constructing new docks downriver at Tilbury. Completed in 1886, but at a cost which far exceeded the estimate, they had little initial success in attracting traffic. The company therefore reduced its charges, inaugurating a competitive battle among the dock companies on the Thames. Despite the investment at Tilbury, there were further attempts to remedy the operating problems at the West India Docks. These included the rebuilding of the Blackwall entrance lock to the Import and Export Docks in 1892–4 and, in 1900–2, another enlargement of the east entrance lock of the South Dock.

Despite further difficulties during the recession in trade that followed the First World War and the later depression, the Port of London Authority, created in 1909 by the amalgamation of the dock companies on the Thames, was able to implement further improvements to the docks. An extensive programme, completed in 1931, included a new South Dock east entrance lock and three passages to link the Millwall, South, Export and Import Docks. These works considerably improved access to the docks, but also reduced berth and shed space. Heavy damage during the Second World War required further reconstruction, although the East India Export Dock, which had been used for the construction of Mulberry floating harbours, was not rebuilt and was gradually filled in.

The immediate post-war period was one of expanding trade and optimism, but by the 1960s it was realized that the India and Millwall Docks were obsolescent. Increasing competition from other British ports, changes in the patterns of world trade, the increasing size of vessels, relative distance from the sea, and, above all, the container revolution in cargo handling all contributed to the change in fortunes of London's up-river docks. The East India Docks closed in 1967, followed by the St Katharine, London, and Surrey Docks in 1968–71. Despite some redevelopment in 1968–70, there was a rapid decline in traffic at the West India and Millwall Docks and they eventually closed in 1980.

The problems of the docks were paralleled by a decline in manufacturing and wharfage, accompanied by a reduction in the number of riverside industrial sites. With the increasing shift to road carriage the river frontage was no longer a locational advantage. The wharves were now of value for the space they provided, not their locations, and the surviving warehouses stored goods brought in by road, rather than by river. Unfortunately, the road connections were inadequate. The decline in the local economy was reflected in a fall in population of 10 per cent between 1961 and 1981.

It was against this background of the closure of the docks, the decline in industry on the Isle of Dogs and the long-term problem of chronically bad road communications that the regeneration of the area was undertaken.

CHAPTER II

The Background to Redevelopment and the Provision of Infrastructure

The beginnings of the process of regeneration in Docklands can be traced to the Greater London Council's plans for the redevelopment of St Katharine's Dock, after its purchase from the Port of London Authority in 1968. Nevertheless, the Council's *Greater London Development Plan* of 1969 failed to foresee the closure of the remainder of London's enclosed docks, and concentrated on plans for the revitalization of riverfront sites throughout London.[1] In 1970 the closure of the London Docks and the Surrey Docks prompted the GLC to consider drawing up strategic plans for the redevelopment of riverside areas east of the Tower, as far as Gravesend and Tilbury. As a first stage, it organized a conference of the various borough and county councils involved, as well as the PLA. In 1971 the Government and the GLC jointly commissioned outside consultants to prepare a Docklands feasibility study, which was published in 1973.[2] In January 1974 the Docklands Joint Committee was set up to take responsibility for planning (development control, strategic plans, and consultation papers) and implementing the redevelopment of London Docklands. It comprised representatives of the GLC and Greenwich, Lewisham, Newham, Southwark, and Tower Hamlets Borough Councils.[3] In 1976 the Joint Committee issued the *London Docklands Strategic Plan*, the basic aim of which was

to use the opportunity provided by large areas of London's Dockland becoming available for development to redress the housing, social, environmental, employment/economic and communications deficiencies of the Docklands area and partner boroughs and thereby to provide the freedom for similar improvements throughout East and Inner London.[4]

The Plan required £1,138 million of public investment to be matched by £600 million of private money,[5] yet it offered no real idea of how the latter would be raised.

The South East Economic Planning Council, an independent body which advised the government, urged – in response to the 1976 Strategic Plan – the setting up of a development corporation, which would be free of political intervention and would be more likely to win the confidence of developers and investors.[6] Such a suggestion was not acceptable to the Labour Government of the day, and Docklands was left to the local authorities, who adopted their normal approach of wide public consultation and much discussion between the different councils and other interested organizations. Progress was inevitably slow, and in 1981 the Conservative Government, seeking to accelerate redevelopment, vested control of the

Docklands area, including the Isle of Dogs, in the London Docklands Development Corporation (LDDC), one of the first two Urban Development Corporations (modelled, as suggested, on those of the New Towns) to be set up as a result of the Local Government and Planning Act of 1980. According to the Act, the object of the Corporation would be

to secure ... regeneration ... by bringing land and buildings into effective use, encouraging the development of existing and new industry and commerce, creating an attractive environment, and ensuring that housing and social facilities are available to encourage people to live and work in the area.[7]

The LDDC was given powers to acquire and dispose of land, as well as responsibility for all planning matters in the Docklands area (6). Enjoying strong government support, the Corporation was not subject to the financial constraints then imposed on local authorities, and did not answer to an electorate.[8]

In 1982 the government designated much of the old docks area as an Enterprise Zone, a move which was to have major repercussions for the redevelopment of part of the Isle of Dogs. This status offered tempting financial incentives to commercial developers and much easier planning processes. The result has been a whirlwind of development producing a physical transformation that has been rapid and spectacular, and is plain to see. What is not yet clear is the lasting effect this will have on the economic and social life of the area.

The Role of the Development Corporation

According to the LDDC's first Chief Architect and Planner, Edward Hollamby:

The great problem for the LDDC was how to obtain quick results, yet set high standards in planning and design. This was necessary if the confidence of the private sector, the public and the Government were to be secured. Such immediacy of action necessarily precluded the lengthy time scale involved in standing back and preparing for an unknown and uncertain future an overall plan.[9]

The LDDC, therefore, eschewed the idea of any sort of master-plan and preferred to rely on market-led redevelopment. Even its design guide for the Isle of Dogs, published in 1982, was quite unlike a normal planning document, for it also showed development opportunities and was not based on precise land-use proposals. The underlying message throughout was that the LDDC's

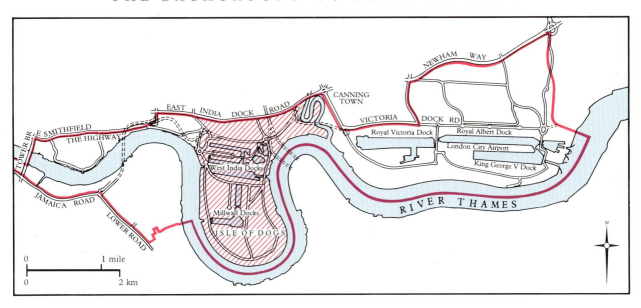

6. The administrative boundary of the London Docklands Development Corporation. Hatching indicates the area covered by this book.

attitude to developments would be flexible and, indeed, the Corporation's chief executive, Reg Ward, later admitted that he stopped the plan from becoming 'prescriptive'.[10] The *Evening Standard*, writing of the mighty Canary Wharf development, argued that 'no docklands plan could have anticipated this event, or allowed the ambitious plans, wildly outside any reasonable expectation, to go ahead'.[11] Such a flexible approach was based on the thesis that conventional land-use planning was inhibiting the entrepreneurial flair and investment necessary to regenerate Britain's run-down industrial and inner-city areas. This argument can be traced back to an article in

New Society in 1969. The question posed was 'what would happen if there were no plan?', and an experiment in 'non-planning' was suggested, the setting up of which would not be difficult legally. 'No land-use pattern could be regarded as sacrosanct' and people would be allowed to build what they liked. Yet the article contained a significant caveat in relation to Docklands: such an experiment could not be tried everywhere, because 'some knots – like London – are, by now, too Gordian for that'.[12]

Although the LDDC was accused of allowing a virtual planning free-for-all in its area, it did involve itself in detailed design matters. At the London Telehouse building,

7. The former No. 30 Shed at West India Docks undergoing demolition in 1989, only six years after its conversion into Limehouse Studios.

for example, it insisted that windows be included for the sake of appearance, although the clients, to maintain secrecy and security, did not wish to have any.[13] At City Harbour the LDDC demanded that plans for a 20-storey hotel (as yet unbuilt) on the edge of the Millwall Dock be amended, after tests suggested that the proposed block would affect sailing and windsurfing in the dock.[14] For Heron Quays, the LDDC approved a new master-plan (revised by the developer in the light of the Canary Wharf proposals) in November 1987, yet a month later decided to replace this with its own master-plan, drawn up by its own architect and outside consultants. The Corporation was able to justify such interference within the Enterprise Zone on the basis that it was the owner of the freehold of the site. Guidelines were given for acceptable heights for buildings, massing and materials. The three different designs subsequently submitted by Scott Brownrigg & Turner on behalf of the developers, Tarmac Brookglade, for the rebuilding of the existing part of the Heron Quays development, were all rejected by the Corporation. The main reason for the rejections seems to have been that the schemes would have been out of harmony with the Canary Wharf scheme, a view supported by the fact that Olympia & York's own master-plan for the eastern part of Heron Quays was approved by the LDDC within four months of submission and before detailed design work had been carried out.[15] At Skylines, the LDDC involved itself in making changes to the winning entry, and also insisted that another developer take over the modified scheme.[16]

The LDDC frequently offered its own sites on a competitive basis. At Caledonian Wharf and Friars Mead it prepared development and layout briefs, and then invited selected developers to submit housing schemes and tender for the site. In the case of Caledonian Wharf the successful developer was Thomas Bates & Sons, whose scheme was designed by Alan Turner & Associates, a combination which had previously been runner-up for another LDDC-owned site elsewhere and had impressed its officers.[17] At Compass Point, the LDDC commissioned Jeremy Dixon and Building Design Partnership to produce designs for a housing scheme, which were incorporated into the tendering documents. Costains, who were the successful tenderers, largely adopted that scheme, although they preferred to use their own staff to execute it (see page 35). At London Yard the LDDC was keen to attract foreign investment, and successfully invited a Dutch-based property group, VOM, to submit a residential scheme for the site (8). In that case the LDDC entered into a related agreement with the developer and with house-purchasers on both land values and purchase prices so that more ambitious landscaping could be provided and larger dwellings than normal could be built for relatively modest prices.[18]

On many of the sites which it owned, the LDDC undertook infrastructure works such as roads and water, gas, electricity and drainage services (as part of a programme to provide a completely new infrastructure for the whole of the Isle of Dogs),[19] and this sometimes involved elab-

8. London Yard, a housing development undertaken after extensive reclamation work by the London Docklands Development Corporation. View looking south-west.

orate and costly works. For instance, on the East India Dock site, where the dock had already been filled in, the LDDC constructed a series of canals to provide a more attractive landscape for subsequent commercial development. At London Yard it spent several million pounds on eradicating methane pollution and on reclamation and river works, so that housing could be built there.[20]

In the 1970s the GLC argued that 'the first condition for a successful comprehensive development of the area must clearly be easier access',[21] while the Docklands Joint Committee regarded public transport 'as the key to the future prosperity of docklands'.[22] The Committee advocated, in the *London Docklands Strategic Plan* (1976), a step-by-step, but concerted, approach to development so that 'at any point there is adequate provision for a viable community to live in the area'. It also pointed out that the large areas of undeveloped land in Docklands offered the opportunity to build and improve roads 'without social disruption on the scale that usually follows in established urban areas'.[23]

In 1980 the Isle of Dogs had no passenger railway and no service by river. A single main road circled its periphery, approached from the congested A13 (East India Dock Road). There were only two bus routes. The improvement of this system, however, presented the classic dilemma of any major reconstruction scheme: whether first to install a massive new transport infrastructure in the hope that subsequent development would justify the expense, or to wait and see what sort of system the actual level of development required. In reality, the LDDC had little choice but to follow the latter course. In the first place, its own decision to rely on market-led development and have no master-plan meant that it was almost impossible, at the outset, to predict traffic needs and levels. As a result the transport infrastructure was installed in a piecemeal fashion and incrementally, and development was allowed to

9. Docklands in the Making: construction work in progress on the east side of Millwall Docks. View from Clippers Quay in 1988.

proceed with little regard for the effect it might have on the transport system.[24] Secondly, in 1980 the Government and the GLC announced that the plans, suggested in the 1976 *Docklands Strategic Plan*, for spending £760 million on new rail and road links for the area, were to be abandoned, and only £100 million would be available for these purposes over the following 15 years. Among the projects cancelled was an extension of the Jubilee Line from Charing Cross to Woolwich.[25] Only very considerable government funding could have provided the new transport system Docklands required, for, as the LDDC admitted, its own public money was 'small in relation to the size of the task'.[26]

The LDDC's initial objective was, therefore, relatively modest: 'to bring the roads and public transport network up to the standard enjoyed in other parts of London.'[27] It went for quickly constructed, apparently cheap solutions: the Docklands Light Railway (DLR) and the 'red brick roads'. But, almost as soon as they were built, they were found to be hopelessly inadequate to cope with the greatly increased amounts of new development.

Nor, in respect of road provision, were the local authorities blameless. Delays in building the Poplar section of the Docklands Highway, vital to easing the congestion on the A13 and providing better access to the Isle of Dogs, were partly due to protracted wrangles between the GLC and Tower Hamlets Borough Council.

To make matters worse, the already inadequate transport system was put under even more pressure as improvements and extensions had to be carried out, during and after the periods of major general development of the area.[28] In 1988, for instance, construction vehicles accounted for about 45 per cent of the new traffic on Docklands roads.[29] In that year there was evidence that potential tenants were being deterred from moving to Docklands because of the transport problems.[30]

It had become obvious that without costly investment in the transport infrastructure the redevelopment of Docklands might flounder. The Government, having persuaded Olympia & York to contribute to the costs of extensions to the DLR and the Jubilee Line, was hopeful that developers might finance all the major transport improvements. However, such an approach was beginning to be regarded as unfair, as it was difficult to identify exactly who the beneficiaries of a particular scheme were or might be in the future. The *Financial Times* concluded that general taxation was often 'the least unfair way' of financing such projects.[31]

Redevelopment had initially been carried out with little apparent cost to the public purse, although generous tax and rate concessions were available within the Enterprise Zone.[a] Up to September 1989, the LDDC had, since its establishment, attracted £6.85 billion in private investment in Docklands, at a cost to itself of only £706 million, raised from government grants and sales of land. By then, however, it had also accumulated a daunting programme of outstanding projects to be funded.

By 1988 the cost of the LDDC's road programme had risen to more than £550 million, nearly three times that estimated when the programme was launched in 1986.[33] The cost of the DLR similarly escalated, from the initial figure of £77 million, to a projected £800 million by 1995 for an expanded network, when the Lewisham extension is built.[34] To signal its concern, the Government, in January 1989, appointed a Minister of State with special responsibility for Docklands transport.[35] In that year the LDDC announced that 'over the next few years the Corporation will spend more than £1 billion, three quarters of which will be invested in new roads and railways'.[36] In view of the LDDC's own financial problems, the Government increased the Corporation's grant for 1989–90 by £91 million to improve the transport infrastructure, chiefly the roads.[37] Indeed, critics have argued that 'the LDDC's approach to transport has been predominantly roads-based, overthrowing the GLC's major roads restraint policy, and is the exception to the general London-wide policy of not building new motorways into the heart of the capital'.[38]

This expenditure came at a time when the LDDC's income from sales of land had drastically dwindled, and the value of the land it still held had fallen steeply. As a result, in 1990, the LDDC went into deficit by £4 million. Following the resignations of several senior officers it reduced its commitments and staffing levels. Nevertheless, for the year ending 31 March 1992, the Corporation showed a deficit of £55 million, and land in Docklands was then valued by the LDDC at only £100,000 an acre, whereas at the height of the boom, in 1988, some sites were fetching as much as £10 million an acre.[39] In February 1991 Eric Sorensen, a civil servant from the Department of the Environment, became its Chief Executive, with the main tasks of completing sales in the Royal Docks and winding up the Corporation in 1998.[40] In October 1990 the Chairman of the LDDC, David Hardy, admitted that the Corporation had learnt the lessons of the Isle of Dogs and was putting infrastructure into the Royal Docks before development began.[41] Shortly afterwards, Michael Heseltine, who had been

responsible for the birth of the Corporation and who was again Secretary of State for the Environment, urged local authorities to join in partnership with the private sector to eradicate 'centres of urban deprivation'.[42]

Roads and Road Transport

The problem of road provision on and to the Isle of Dogs was particularly difficult. The creation of new roads, especially through the densely populated areas at the northwestern approaches, would arouse political, social and environmental controversies. In addition, no one authority had overall responsibility. Some new roads were privately built as part of individual development schemes, while others were built by the LDDC to open up the area to development. More major roads, providing access to the Island, were the responsibility of the GLC until its demise in 1986, while the principal strategic routes, such as the A13, came under the Department of Transport.[43]

The LDDC constructed a new public road, Marsh Wall, at a cost of £2½ million, in order to give entry into the heart of the formerly enclosed docks area and the newly designated Enterprise Zone. Opened in 1983, it was three-quarters of a mile long, and ran from Westferry Road, through the site of the main gate of the West India Docks, round the south-west corner of the South West India Dock, and between the West India and Millwall Docks, to join Manchester Road on the eastern side of the Island (*10*). It was dubbed the 'red brick road' because it was paved with over two million 'bricks' (actually red concrete blocks), laid in herringbone fashion, for ease and cheapness of maintenance.[44] At the same time, shorter but similarly constructed roads – Lighterman's Road, Limeharbour, Mastmaker Road and Millharbour – were opened to give access off Marsh Wall to development sites on either side of the Millwall Dock.

All of these roads were so narrow that two-way traffic could not pass parked vehicles, and they were built to cope with the traffic generated by between five and eight million sq.ft of commercial space, whereas by 1988 a total of about 25 million sq.ft was planned.[45] The LDDC, therefore, had to carry out improvements to these roads between 1989 and 1991, at an estimated cost of £5 million.[46] Also, Marsh Wall was reconstructed so that its north-western end terminated at Westferry Circus.[47]

Improving access to the Isle of Dogs was more difficult and took much longer to accomplish. The necessary widening of the northern ends of the two main roads to the Island, Westferry and Preston's Roads, was not carried out until the second half of the 1980s.[48] More serious was the delay in constructing a major new road to the north of the Isle of Dogs, which would both provide a southern relief route to the heavily congested East India Dock Road (A13) and give better access to the Island. Such a road had been proposed by the GLC in the 1970s and early 1980s, but the precise route was the source of

---

[a] In 1989 the *Economist* estimated that the rates concessions in the Enterprise Zone were running at about £24 million a year, while the tax concessions granted up to 1992 would, on the basis of development committed, cost the Government about £1.5 billion.[32]

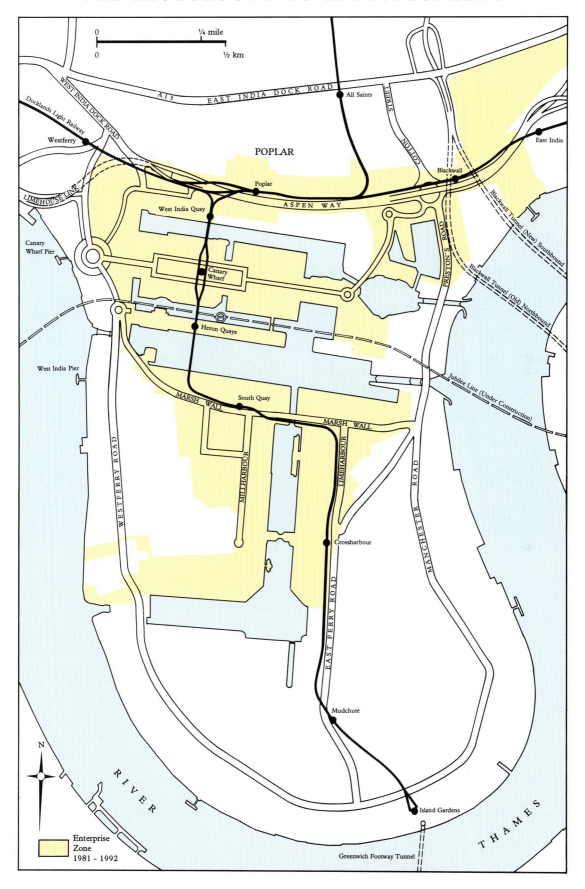

10. The railways and principal roads on the Isle of Dogs, 1995.

considerable disagreement between the GLC and Tower Hamlets Borough Council.[49] In the event, this scheme was superseded by the more ambitious 'Docklands Highway' proposed by the LDDC to run from Wapping to the Royal Docks.[50] The Poplar section was built in three parts: the Limehouse, East India, and Poplar Links, all of which were completed in 1993 (*10*). The last linked the other two, and merely extended and widened the western section of Aspen Way, built by the LDDC in about 1987.[51]

The Limehouse Link, from The Highway to Westferry Road, was approved in principle in 1986. The initial estimate was £41 million, but the successful tender, announced in September 1989, from Balfour Beatty in association with Fairclough, was £171 million. The decision to build this 1.8km-long road in a tunnel added considerably to the cost and was made largely on environmental grounds, as the road runs through densely populated housing estates. Delays in handing over land to contractors, unforeseen problems with soil conditions, and stricter than expected noise abatement requirements led to further increases in the costs of the road, which by October 1992 were said to be about £345 million (including rehousing and the purchase of the land). Early in 1992 the LDDC took over direct management of the construction of the scheme, bringing in engineers from the American firm of Bechtel. The Limehouse Link was opened by the Prime Minister, John Major, in May 1993. Its western portal is decorated by a mural sculpture, 'Restless Dream', by Zadoc Ben-David, while further sculptures, both untitled, by Michael Kenny and Nigel Hall adorn respectively the eastern portals to the Isle of Dogs and to Aspen Way (*12*).[52]

For the East India Dock Link, a contract worth £32 million to construct the 1km-long dual carriageway and the associated Preston's Road flyover was awarded by the LDDC to Edmund Nuttall Ltd in November 1990.[53] This section of the road supersedes the eastern section of Aspen Way, which was built in 1987–9 by Wimpey for the LDDC at a cost of £6.9 million.[54] Near the site of Brunswick Wharf Power Station the East India Dock Link divides. One part runs north-east to join the A13, and is in a 350m-long tunnel which avoids compromising development along the line of the road, particularly the former East India Import Dock site.[55] The other part continues eastwards to link with the Leamouth roundabout and the Lower Lea Crossing, designed to give a direct connection between the Isle of Dogs and the Royal Docks.[56]

Docklands Light Railway

In 1967 a monorail was suggested as an alternative to an underground railway as a means of improving Docklands transport and of boosting commercial growth in the area. It was pointed out that the tracks of the former Broad Street to the Isle of Dogs railway could be utilized, and a further line from South London to Stratford was envisaged.[57] In 1973 a study team, commissioned jointly by the GLC and the Department of the Environment to draw up redevelopment proposals for East London, suggested a rapid transit route through Docklands, employing 'minitrams', running under automatic control and operating on much sharper track alignments than a conventional railway.[58]

Despite the urgings of the Light Railway Transport League,[59] the 1976 *London Docklands Strategic Plan*, produced by the Docklands Joint Committee, was rather wary of any tramway or light rapid transit scheme, being particularly concerned about the technical and operational problems.[60] Nevertheless, the shelving of plans to extend the Jubilee underground line forced the GLC, in conjunction with the LDDC, to explore low-cost alternatives. As a result, in June 1982 *Public Transport Provision for Docklands* – a report jointly prepared by the LDDC, the GLC, London Transport, and the Departments of Transport, the Environment and Industry – advocated the construction of two new light-railway routes, totalling about 7½ miles. A quick decision was required and the Government responded remarkably rapidly, agreeing to provide the £77 million needed to establish the railway. London Transport, on behalf of the GLC and the LDDC, was responsible for preparing the Parliamentary plans, and constructing and running the railway.[b] Parliamentary approval for the Docklands Light Railway (DLR) route from Tower Hill to the Isle of Dogs was received in April 1984, and that from Poplar to Stratford in April 1985.[61] Such a railway could be built cheaply and quickly, while its innovative nature ensured extensive publicity. Thus, given the need to attract developers to a poorly served area, the DLR seemed to offer 'a credible, high-profile passenger transport system with an air of permanence and reliability, free of the notorious congestion of some East End roads'.[62]

In advance of Parliamentary approval, Arup Associates, as design consultants, in conjunction with Design House, Pentagram, G. Maunsell & Partners, Kennedy & Donkin, and Henderson Busby, had, from April 1983, been producing detailed designs and specifications for signs, trains, stations and structures. The contract, valued at £58.4 million, to design (using the Arup team's proposals as guidelines), build and equip the DLR was awarded to a consortium of GEC and John Mowlem in August 1984, and construction began in that year.[63] The railway was officially opened by the Queen on 30 July 1987, but, because of safety problems, the first public trains did not run until 31 August.[64]

Strictly, the DLR is not a light railway but a fully fledged one. Nevertheless, the system is entirely separate from both those of British Rail and London Underground, and does not have to conform to their standards. It operates on much sharper bends, for example, and the trains are more akin to trams than to conventional railway carriages.

---

[b] Docklands Light Railway Ltd was a wholly owned subsidiary of London Regional Transport.

11. The north-eastern approaches to the Isle of Dogs. The Beckton extension of the Docklands Light Railway and the East India Dock Link looking towards Preston's Road flyover at dusk.

The DLR uses standard-gauge track, and electric power is supplied at 750 volts direct current from a low-level third rail. All trains are automatically driven and controlled by a central computer at Poplar. No drivers are required, but there is a 'Train Captain' who controls the opening and closing of doors at stations, and can, in certain circumstances, manually drive the train.[65]

Lines from Tower Gateway and Stratford and Beckton meet just north of West India Quay station, and the southern terminus is at Island Gardens (*10*). The route through the Isle of Dogs betrays the fact that the DLR was meant to serve the commercial developments within the Enterprise Zone, rather than those of the residential areas around the periphery of the Island.

Approximately two-thirds of the first phase of the DLR was built on disused or under-used railway lines. East of Limehouse it is carried on the former London and Blackwall Railway viaduct, built in 1840, and south of Mudchute station on a 27-arch viaduct built in 1872 and totally disused since 1926. New bridges, utilizing specially fabricated 65m-wide steel spans, carry the railway over the three West India docks.[66] Earlier schemes for a Docklands railway had envisaged tunnelling under the docks, but their closure made bridging possible. The dramatic way in which the railway crossed the water drew attention to its presence in the heart of the Enterprise Zone.[67]

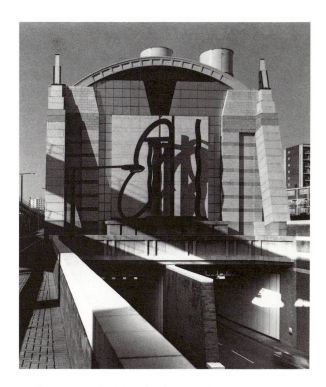

12. Eastern portal of the Limehouse Link road tunnel with its untitled sculpture by Nigel Hall.

13. A Docklands Light Railway train sweeps dramatically round a curved reflective glass wall at Harbour Exchange.

14. The Docklands Light Railway terminus at Island Gardens.

The stations closely follow the designs suggested by Arup and their collaborators. They relied on a 'kit of parts' approach, employing standard prefabricated components to provide only very basic facilities, which could be improved as the need arose and finance permitted.[68] Platforms were initially 30m long, with simple bus-shelter-type canopies, which have curved tops. They are made of metal and are glazed with polycarbonate.[69] The terminus at Island Gardens is more elaborate, with a domed staircase-tower which echoes that of the nearby Greenwich Foot Tunnel (*14*).[70] The grandest of all is the station at Canary Wharf, protected by an overall roof (see page 64) (*16*). The stations have ticket-vending machines at street level.[71]

Even as the DLR was being built, the vast number of jobs expected to be created by the Canary Wharf development rendered the railway incapable of coping with the predicted quantities of passengers (from an original estimate of 1,500 per hour, to 13,000 per hour).[72] In June 1987, therefore, even before the railway was officially opened, a contract worth £50 million was awarded to GEC-Mowlem to carry out immediate improvements. These included new trains, the lengthening of platforms to allow double-length trains, and additional track facilities at Canary Wharf.[73] The first of the double-length trains came into service in February 1991.[74]

After its opening the DLR was beset with operating difficulties.[75] These were partly due to the innovative nature of the system, and its technical complexities. For example, any failure of the central computer brought the whole system to a standstill.[76] Its very success added to the problems, for it was almost overwhelmed by the numbers of passengers. In particular, its popularity with tourists, who were curious to see the new system or who used it as a route to Greenwich, seems to have been grossly underestimated.[77] By 1989, well before the opening of Canary Wharf, the DLR was carrying 30,000 passengers a day,[78] whereas the original forecast had been a maximum of 22,000 a day by 1991.[79] The work required to improve and extend the railway in itself caused considerable disruption to the existing services.[80]

The advantage of linking Canary Wharf to the heart of the City with a new DLR terminus at Bank underground station was recognized in the *Public Transport Provision for Docklands* (1982). The provision of this link was one of the requirements of the developers of Canary Wharf from the earliest days, under G. Ware Travelstead (see page 53).[81] Such a link was psychologically important as Canary Wharf was being promoted as an extension of, or even an alternative to, the City.[82] Parliamentary approval was granted in 1986 and Olympia & York, having taken over the Canary Wharf development, agreed to pay a half of the original estimated cost of £150 million, with the Government providing the remainder.[83] Work began in that year, a limited service began in July 1991 and the work was completed by the end of that year.[84]

Work began on a further 8km-long extension, to the Royal Docks at Beckton, in 1989.[85] It was designed by G. Maunsell & Partners, with architectural design by Ahrends, Burton & Koralek.[86] The estimated cost of

15. A night-time view of the footbridge over Aspen Way connecting North Quay with the Docklands Light Railway station at Poplar *(right)*.

£240 million was paid by the LDDC, with funding provided entirely by the Government, after private developers had declined to provide financial support.[87] The section between West India Dock Road and Preston's Road, including the reconstruction of Poplar station (with a footbridge to North Quay, opened in October 1992) (15), was carried out by Balfour Beatty, at a cost of £22 million, while construction of the main section from Preston's Road to Beckton (involving a new Blackwall station at Preston's Road) was carried out by a combination of Mowlem and Taylor Woodrow for £116 million. The Beckton extension came into service in March 1994.[88]

In November 1990 the Transport Secretary announced the intention to build a 2.3-mile southern extension to the DLR, running under the Thames to Greenwich and Lewisham, but he insisted that the £130-million scheme was to be built and operated by the private sector.[89] Although work was expected to start in 1992, the Bill authorizing the line did not receive the Royal Assent until the summer of 1993,[90] and work is now scheduled to start in 1996, with completion in 1999.[91]

In 1991 work began on a project costing £8 million to add two further tracks between North Quay and Canary Wharf, which also involved rebuilding West India Quay station. The main contractor was Mowlem Civil Engineering and the work was completed in 1993.[92]

Following Ministerial complaints and lobbying from Olympia & York, in April 1992 ownership of the DLR was transferred from London Transport to the LDDC.[93] The figures for March to May 1992 showed that reliability had greatly improved and in one week the DLR had the best reliability figure for any railway line in London. In the same period passenger numbers rose to 32,000 a day, having fallen to 23,000 in 1991.[94] By 1995, the railway was carrying 50,000 passengers a day, with 98 per cent of trains running to schedule.[95]

The Jubilee Line Extension

Proposals for an eastward extension to the Jubilee underground line had long existed, and the original intention was that it should include links with Cannon Street and Fenchurch Street stations.[96] However, a report published by London Transport International in 1988 suggested that the Jubilee Line extension was neither an immediate priority for London's overall transport network nor even for that of Docklands.[97] Nevertheless, Olympia & York, pressed by some of their future tenants, considered the extension vital to the success of Canary Wharf, and during 1988 and early 1989 attempted to introduce a Private Bill into Parliament authorizing the line.[98] When this failed, they approached the Government, offering to raise £180 million from private sources towards the cost of construction, then put at £450 million (as against £230 million in 1980).[99] In November 1989 approval was given for a ten-mile extension of the Jubilee Line, from Green Park via Waterloo and London Bridge to Canary Wharf and Stratford. But the Government made it clear that any extension would only be built if there was 'a very sub-

stantial contribution from private developers'.[100] The developers (mainly, in fact, Olympia & York) agreed to contribute £400 million over 25 years towards the estimated cost, now £1 billion.[101] When the developers of Port Greenwich offered to contribute £25 million, the route was altered in 1990 to run southwards via that development rather than eastwards through the East India Dock site.[102] The Bill for the Jubilee Line extension was submitted in November 1989,[103] but was not approved until March 1992.[104] With Olympia & York already in financial difficulties, its bankers were unwilling to sanction the payment of the company's initial contribution of £40 million due on 1 April 1992 (see page 59).[105] In November 1992 it was announced that the Government had negotiated a satisfactory arrangement for the funding of the project.[106] It is to provide £1.5 billion for the project and Canary Wharf's bankers the other £400 million. Work on the extension began in December 1993, and the line is due to open in 1998. The new Jubilee Line station at Canary Wharf has been designed by Sir Norman Foster & Partners.[107]

Docklands River Bus

In 1973 the London Docklands Study Team argued that river transport could not be a major contributor to public transport for Docklands, because of its limited capacity and the difficulties of providing satisfactory links with other forms of public transport.[108] Nevertheless, the GLC and the LDDC explored the possibilities of introducing such a service.[109] A trial service using one boat began in the summer of 1987,[110] operated by Thames Line, a private company set up under the Government's Business Expansion scheme, whereby individuals could claim tax relief on amounts invested in the company.[111] A regular service commenced in June 1988, using 62-seater catamarans, powered by water-jet. Initially these operated from Charing Cross and were capable of covering the journey to West India Pier in 20 minutes. The service was extended westwards to Chelsea Harbour in September 1988, and southwards to Greenwich in 1989.[112] Following the opening of Canary Wharf to the public in late July 1991, the River Bus used the new Canary Wharf Pier instead of West India Pier (10).[113]

Within six months of commencing regular services, Thames Line was experiencing operating problems and financial difficulties. The service needed to carry about 20,000 passengers a week to break even, but attracted only about 5,000, as too few people were then working in Docklands, the fares were relatively high, and, until the service was extended to Greenwich, there was little tourist traffic.[114]

Between 1989 and 1993 several financial rescues were mounted by a series of consortia formed by companies involved in Docklands, the LDDC, and local authorities.[115] Despite these efforts, the River Bus was said to have lost £2 million in 1992, and the service ceased abruptly in August 1993, when the operating company went into liquidation.[116]

16. The soaring roof spanning the Docklands Light Railway station at Canary Wharf (see page 64).

Key

17. Modern Docklands: the Enterprise Zone and new developments on the Isle of Dogs, 1981-95.

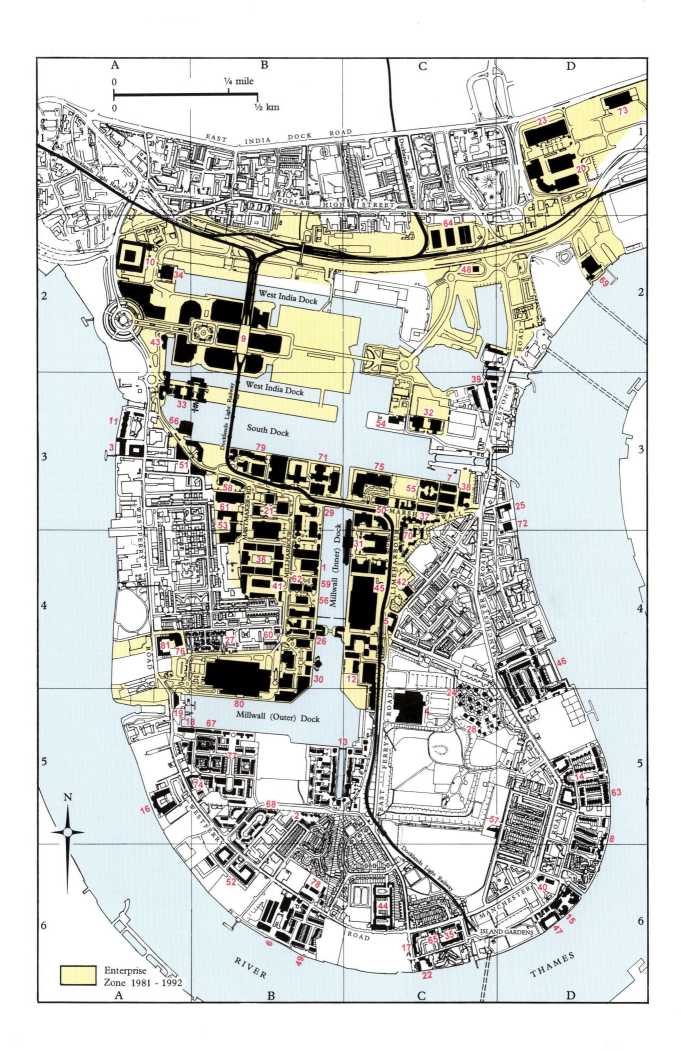

Enterprise
Zone 1981 - 1992

Docklands Housing

The dwellings built during the Docklands period of the 1980s and early 1990s have produced what may be regarded as a third major phase of housing on the Isle of Dogs. Industrial development around the riverfront during the early nineteenth century was accompanied by the construction of working-class houses, most of them in plain terraces. On the Millwall side of the Island this was a gradual and patchy process. It was no less sluggish on the eastern side, in Cubitt Town, despite a coherent programme of development in the 1840s during which the foreshore was embanked and the principal streets were set out. Even there, building was slow and only accelerated into a veritable boom in the early 1860s. This was brought to an abrupt halt by the effects of the financial crash of 1866, which produced high levels of unemployment and much distress. There was some further building in the late nineteenth century, but few private houses were erected thereafter and the first phase of housing came to an end around the turn of the century. The second phase saw the construction of public housing by the local authorities and housing associations, initially on a small scale, but eventually replacing almost all of the small and often inadequate houses that were characteristic of the earlier phase. Widespread destruction during the Second World War acted as a catalyst to this process: in Cubitt Town the number of houses fell from more than 1,600 in 1937 to fewer than 700 in 1948. Much of the public housing was constructed during the 1960s and 1970s, but the local authorities ceased to erect dwellings in the early 1980s and the housing associations could only build on a comparatively small scale.

By 1970 there was little private housing on the Isle of Dogs, but something of a revival began in the next few years, with the construction of small-scale developments at Nos 71–91 (odd) Saunders Ness Road (1972) and Capstan Square, off Stewart Street (1974). Capstan

18. Aerial view of Clippers Quay, an early Docklands housing development begun in 1984, and laid out around the former graving dock at the Millwall Docks (see page 35).

Square was also representative of a trend to use riverside sites for housing, a process that had begun in the mid-1930s with two blocks built by the LCC at Phoenix Wharf, close to the Millwall Docks entrance, and had continued with several larger public housing developments in Cubitt Town during the 1970s and early 1980s.

The Background

As far as the local authorities were concerned, the closure of the docks provided an opportunity to use the dock estate to meet the housing needs of the local people. The 1976 *London Docklands Strategic Plan* recognized the need to extend the range of tenure in the area, but argued that simply to introduce private housing would not help most of those in need, because it would be beyond their economic means. For Tower Hamlets, therefore, the plan tentatively suggested that while 40 per cent of new Docklands housing should be local authority and 20 per cent should be for owner occupation, a further 40 per cent should have some form of 'middle tenure', such as equity-sharing, housing association, or co-operative schemes.[1] Tower Hamlets Borough Council's own plan for the Isle of Dogs, published in 1981, broadly endorsed the views of the 1976 joint plan, but emphasized that in any new housing development programme 'there should be a high proportion of local authority and housing association developments'.[2] As a result of the 1976 plan, between that date and 1981 some 1,300 houses were built in Docklands and in 1981 another 900 were under construction, mostly for rent.[3]

One immediate result of the setting up of the LDDC was that it acquired more than 600 acres of public land, mostly owned by the local authorities and intended for public housing.[4] Although apparently there were some initial thoughts that the LDDC might build houses itself, to set a standard and encourage developers to follow its example, private house-builders quickly came forward and made this unnecessary.[5] In its public pronouncements the Corporation emphasized that it was not a housing authority and had no remit to build houses. Nevertheless, it did have a housing role, which was primarily to provide sites for development by private builders or by housing associations. According to the Secretary of State for the Environment in July 1980, the LDDC could, when disposing of such sites, impose conditions on the developers, which 'might specify the type of housing to be provided or the purchase price, and might give nomination rights either to LDDC or to the local housing authority, enabling preference to be given to those in housing need, key workers etc.'.[6]

In fact, the LDDC saw one of its objectives as being to 'help a faster council building rate', and in 1986 stated that it had offered land for house building to Newham, Southwark, and Tower Hamlets Borough Councils. It went on, however, to say that 'because the authorities are having problems allocating the necessary cash to develop them, the LDDC will help in creating partnership arrangements between the councils and private develop-

ers to build mixed schemes for rent and sale'.[7] Shortly afterwards, 'social housing' began to be considered in government circles as an alternative to local authority housing and the concept was eagerly taken up by the Corporation. The term, which originated on the Continent, tends to be applied to housing schemes subsidized by agencies other than local authorities and designed to provide rented accommodation or a home for sale for those on lower incomes who would otherwise not be able to afford such property: for example, housing association, co-operative, equity-sharing, and self-build schemes, or a combination of those elements. Housing associations' involvement in social housing had been facilitated by the fact that since 1980 they had been able to provide houses for sale through special low-cost schemes, such as shared ownership. One result of all this on the Isle of Dogs is the Masthouse Terrace project (*19*), where funding has come partly from the East London Housing Association, with the assistance of a grant given by the LDDC, and partly from a private loan, while some of the site has been donated by Tower Hamlets Borough Council and the rest purchased from the Development Corporation (see page 43).

19. Phoenix Court, Masthouse Terrace, Westferry Road, a collaborative scheme involving a housing association, the Borough Council and the London Docklands Development Corporation (see page 43).

In addition, the LDDC had the stated role 'to help improve older council housing so that living standards are raised for more people and new homes more quickly integrated into the existing community'.[8] Initially, however, it felt constrained to fund only environmental improvements around individual blocks or estates, or community projects.[9] During 1987 and 1988 the Corporation explored ways of assisting with the external and internal refurbishment of the actual buildings on the Council's

20. Urmston and Salford Houses, Seyssel Street, early 1960s
LCC flats reclad in Docklands fashion in the early 1990s.

estates, although the costs of the Docklands Highway initially absorbed the money earmarked by the Corporation for those purposes.[10] In 1988 the Corporation appointed a Director of Community Services (whose remit included housing)[11] and, in the following year, a Housing Refurbishment Manager, to liaise with local authorities and to secure funding for refurbishment programmes.[12] The Corporation's *Housing Strategy Review* gave a programme for the three financial years from 1990 to 1993, totalling £3 million for refurbishment to housing on the Isle of Dogs.[13] As a result, housing blocks on some council estates have been completely reclad and have the appearance of modern private developments (20).

In terms of land use and geography, the new housing of Docklands followed the pattern set in the 1970s and early 1980s by a series of housing schemes (instigated by various agencies), in being built on redundant wharves and industrial sites on the east side of the Isle of Dogs; indeed, those sites were suggested for residential development in Tower Hamlets Borough Council's Isle of Dogs plan.[14] Of the 12 housing schemes begun after the inception of the LDDC and before the end of 1986, nine were on the eastern half of the Island, and six of these were built on former industrial riverside sites. The 14 schemes begun between 1987 and 1990 show an almost complete reversal, with only four on the east side of the Island and ten on the west side – where the London Borough of Tower Hamlets had wished to retain sites in industrial use[15] – and a total of only five riverside sites (although there are permissions for residential developments on several more, not yet implemented). In part this reflects the fact that as the price of land in Docklands rose the ex-

isting industrial firms on the west side of the Island were more ready to relocate elsewhere and sell their old sites for residential development. The designation in 1982 of the land immediately around the docks as an Enterprise Zone offering tax and rate concessions to business developments had the effect of virtually excluding new housing from that area. For this reason only three of the housing developments built up to 1992 actually had dockside locations.

'Affordable' Homes

The type of tenure of the new housing was very different from that already built or envisaged by the local authorities. One of the assumptions behind the LDDC's housing policy was that it needed to provide dwellings for sale in order to help redress the apparent imbalance created by the presence of so much council-owned, rented accommodation in the area.[16] According to the LDDC's own figures, from 1982 until 31 March 1988, of a total of 2,819 housing starts on the Isle of Dogs, 2,737 were for sale, 22 were for shared ownership, and only 60 were available for renting.[17] While, for Docklands as a whole, between 1981 and 1991 the proportion of owner-occupier households rose from 5 per cent to 38 per cent and the proportion of households living in local authority dwellings had dropped from 83 per cent to 39 per cent.[18]

Nevertheless, one of the LDDC's roles was to improve conditions for the existing population and it sought to ensure that a reasonable proportion of the new housing would be occupied by local people. On a number of developments on the Isle of Dogs, therefore, priority was given to local applicants living in rented accommodation. In several instances the Corporation also required that a certain number of dwellings in a scheme should be 'affordable' housing – the Corporation's definition of affordable being below £40,000. On the Isle of Dogs, the Glengall Place and Friars Mead schemes were intended to provide affordable housing, and in 1984 and 1985 two-bedroom houses could be obtained on those developments for no more than £37,000. On the more desirable dockside or riverside sites the LDDC allowed developers to charge high prices for the best positions overlooking the water in return for offering the rest of the housing at affordable prices.[19] Thus, in 1984 a two-bedroom flat could be obtained at Clippers Quay for £39,495,[20] while even in 1986 properties for £40,000 or less were available on the riverside developments at Caledonian Wharf, Compass Point and London Yard (21).[21]

However, as house prices in Docklands rapidly escalated, so the proportion of affordable new dwellings dropped. For example, on sites owned by the LDDC, by September 1985, 74 per cent of the dwellings sold cost less than £40,000, but by the end of 1987 only 42 per cent were at an affordable figure,[22] and only 12 per cent of those went to former council tenants.[23] The rapid rise in house prices also meant, of course, that dwellings originally offered at affordable levels were well above the £40,000 mark when they were resold.[24] Indeed, in 1988

21. Caledonian Wharf, a riverside housing development which included some 'affordable homes' (see page 33).

the Corporation had to admit 'it is increasingly difficult, if not impossible, for homes to be offered at "affordable" prices',[25] and in 1989 the affordable-homes scheme was abandoned in favour of the 'social' housing programme mentioned above.[26]

Docklands-based groups argued that these policies of local priority and affordable prices were of little use to those already living in the area, and in any case were subject to widespread abuse. A dwelling of £40,000 was beyond the means of many local people and ignored the need for more rented accommodation. It was said that people outside the area gave local addresses to qualify for priority, that tenants sold their rent books to others, and that the policy, however well intentioned, allowed speculators to acquire cheap dwellings which they never occupied and sold on for a quick profit.[27] While not denying that the local-priority system had been abused, the LDDC disputed that such abuse was as widespread as alleged.[28] Nevertheless, at the end of 1985, in an attempt to deter speculators, it did tighten up the system, requiring, among other things, purchasers who resold within five years to pay back a proportion of any profit made.[29] In 1990 the LDDC claimed that 58 per cent of those who

had moved to live in Docklands since 1981 had come from Docklands boroughs.[30] On the other hand, in 1991 a report that was critical of the LDDC claimed that only 2,253 of the 15,200 flats and houses built in Docklands since 1981 had been for local people.[31]

Development and Design

Of the 26 housing schemes to be built on the Isle of Dogs between 1981 and 1992, only six were actually on land owned by the LDDC and all were begun in the mid-1980s. On two of these, at the Mudchute and Maconochie's Wharf, self-build schemes were carried out, and in both instances those promoting the projects made the first approach to the Corporation. Of the private developers responsible for residential schemes on the Isle of Dogs, Kentish Property Group was the only one which specialized in Docklands projects. The firm had already been active in East London with a number of residential schemes, either involving the conversion of old buildings or the erection of new ones. Its Cascades development on the Island seemed a brilliant success[a] and in the summer of 1987 the company was able to make a share-issue valued at £37 million.[33] It then set about converting and re-developing Burrell's Wharf, but this was to prove its downfall (see page 32).

The overwhelming majority of housing schemes built under the LDDC regime have been developed by the national, volume house-builders such as Barratts, Wates, Costains, Fairclough, Groveside Homes, Ideal Homes, Laing and Wimpey. This was probably due in part to the fact that Sir Nigel Broackes and his next two successors as chairman of the LDDC, Christopher Benson and David Hardy, all came from the property industry.[34] In stylistic terms, some of the house-builders have made little concession to the area and have been content to employ their own standard dwelling-types (22). Most, though, have engaged outside architects to design

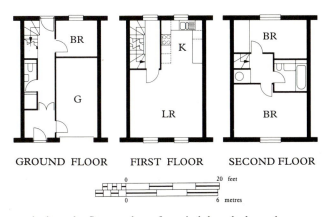

GROUND FLOOR   FIRST FLOOR   SECOND FLOOR

22. Ambassador Square, plans of a typical three-bedroom house. Developed by Laing Homes using their standard dwelling types (see page 32).

[a] In fact, apartments were still being heavily marketed in July 1992, as the result of repossessions in the previous year, and it was still thought worthwhile to maintain a show flat in January 1993.[32]

23. Fast-track building: Cascades apartment block under construction in 1987 (see page 34).

touches, usually metal balconies with brightly painted railings and an occasional 'porthole' window. Only The Anchorage and Cascades exhibit a more full-blooded treatment in this style, however (*Frontispiece, 24, 34*). At least five developments (Felstead Gardens, Glengall Bridge, Jamestown Harbour, Luralda Gardens and Plymouth Wharf) have blocks which seek to re-create the appearance of traditional riverside and dockside warehouses. Beginning with Compass Point, a number of housing schemes have, to varying degrees, Classical aspirations. Compass Point and De Bruin Court are more Regency in feel (*25*), while parts of Timber Wharves employ a reworking of the traditional Georgian-London terraced house, and Lockes Field attempts to re-create an eighteenth-century mews (*43*). The layouts at Compass Point and Timber Wharves are also Classically inspired and both have an impressive central axis (*28*). However, apart from Lockes Field, the other three developments all have touches of Modernism as well.

Some of these schemes were designed very defensively, most notably at Luralda Gardens, where the closed gates are apparently guarded by two gatehouses (which actually each contain a studio-flat), and at Cumberland Mills, where there is a sophisticated television surveillance system with a control centre by the entrance gates (again normally shut), which is manned continuously. It is not clear whether these installations were just part of the general demand for protection against crime and vandalism,

schemes specifically for particular sites. Nevertheless, in comparison with the new commercial developments on the Isle of Dogs, the housing has – apart from a few exceptions – been quite conservative in design, and there are rather more traditional-style houses than might be expected. Materials have tended to be equally traditional: walls faced in red, brown, yellow, or buff brick, often relieved by dressings in a contrasting colour; pitched or hipped roofs covered in slates (albeit often artificial) or tiles. Construction methods have also generally been conventional, partly because many developers acted as their own building contractors, although both Cascades and Cyclops Wharf employed 'fast-track' methods, pioneered in North America, which made extensive use of precast concrete and prefabricated components. At Cascades, a central concrete core was constructed to the full 20 storeys, and structural floor-slabs were then cast from the bottom up (*23*). Not only was the system fast (Cascades was completed in just over 18 months), but floors could be occupied as they were completed, and while work on the upper floors continued.[35] Another device adopted to speed up building work at Cascades and The Anchorage was the installation of complete, prefabricated bathrooms (fully fitted, even to the tiles on the walls).[36]

The presence of the river and the docks had a powerful influence on the design of much of the housing. Few designers were able to resist at least one or two 'nautical'

24. Docklands Nautical: The Anchorage, looking north (see page 32).

25. Docklands Regency: the quadrant at the west end of Sextant Avenue (see page 35).

26. Waterside lifestyle 1: Clippers Quay, Millwall Docks, houses with boat moorings in the former graving dock. View looking south-east (see page 35).

or were more specifically intended as a defence against the supposed threat of local hostility, fuelled by newspaper stories at the time. Certainly, in 1989 security was a major concern of would-be purchasers on the Isle of Dogs.[37]

So far, most of these developments have been exclusively residential, another result, to some extent, of the designation of the Enterprise Zone. The major exception is Glengall Bridge, conceived as a 'Business Village', a mixed development of residential, commercial and retail space. This was, indeed, the only new housing built within the Enterprise Zone. Otherwise three housing schemes also included some shops (Cascades, Cyclops Wharf and London Yard – where there is also a restaurant), while The Anchorage incorporated four commercial units, and the Burrell's Wharf scheme was also intended to have a number of business and commercial units.[38] These last two, together with Cascades and Cyclops Wharf, offered leisure centres as an integral part of their schemes.

Selling Docklands

The LDDC, the developers and estate agents engaged in a high-powered marketing campaign which received widespread coverage in the media and was designed to persuade house-buyers to come to Docklands, more especially to the Isle of Dogs. The proximity of the river and the docks influenced not only design, but was also seen as a major marketing feature. An image was presented of residents mooring their motor boats or yachts alongside their homes, and indulging in water sports such as sailboarding and water-skiing. Similarly, the names given to these Docklands housing schemes usually invoke a waterside connection: 'Quay' and 'Wharf' are the most favoured, but there is also London Yard (the former name of the site) and Jamestown Harbour (a new name), as well as the more obviously nautical The Anchorage and

Compass Point (where the old name of Dudgeon's Wharf could hardly have appealed to a developer). In fact, all this is fairly illusory. Most of the riverside sites have no direct access to the river and, as already mentioned, only three housing developments enjoy dockside situations. In any case, the tidal nature and fast currents of the river and the state of the water in the docks can make leisure activities dangerous,[39] while until the completion of the Docklands Sailing Centre in 1989 there was little in the way of facilities for water sports. Even on a development such as Clippers Quay, with its own private moorings, scarcely any boats are actually to be found there (18, 26). Surprisingly, a survey taken in 1988 revealed that the presence of water was not the most significant attraction for most Docklands home-buyers.[40]

The Island is only about 2½ miles from the heart of the City, and this was another selling-point for houses in Docklands. The 'Big Bang' of October 1986 (see page 48) in the City created a large potential house-buying market of highly paid workers seeking to live close to the City[41] – many of them young and, in social terms, upwardly mobile (the so-called 'yuppies'). However, the notoriously inadequate road and rail systems made the Isle of Dogs less immediately accessible to the City than its position suggested. Nevertheless, the 1988 survey indicated that about half of the house-buyers in Wapping, Surrey Docks and the Isle of Dogs were professionals or worked in the City, and their main reason for living in Docklands was its proximity to the City or their place of work.[42]

So, Docklands was promoted as offering a luxurious way of life, aimed especially at City 'whizz-kids' looking to enjoy the fruits of their hard work and wanting relaxation from their hectic lifestyles – hence the attraction of glamorous water sports and the inclusion on a number of the later developments of leisure centres. The extensive media coverage helped to suggest that Docklands was the fashionable place to live. The dwellings themselves were

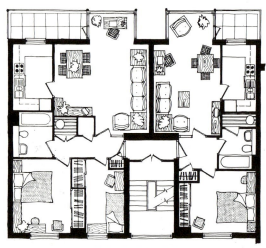

FIRST FLOOR

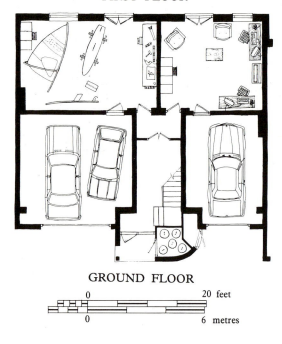

GROUND FLOOR

0   20 feet

0   6 metres

27. Waterside lifestyle 2: plans of one- and two-bedroom flats
at Jamestown Harbour, as envisaged by the developers
(see page 39).

promoted as the last word in luxury, but this claim did not always bear close scrutiny. In 1989, when large numbers of new homes were still empty, housing associations began to consider taking them over but found that many were below their normal standards.[43] Of all the recent housing, Cascades was the most explicit and most successful in promoting an image of unashamed luxury. Purchasers of apartments there were less impressed when they subsequently found that some dwellings in the block were being rented to people receiving housing benefit,[44] while the majority of dwellings at Timber Wharves were occupied by council tenants rehoused from the St Vincent Estate, Limehouse.

A Speculators' Market

Another major incentive for house-buyers, until 1988 at least, was that dwellings on the Isle of Dogs seemed to offer a profitable investment.[45] The initial development of Docklands coincided with a rapid increase in house prices in London and the South East, but those in Docklands – including the Isle of Dogs – rose more dramatically than anywhere else in London, except Westminster.[46] Indeed, house prices on the Island between 1985 and 1987 far outstripped the hopes of the most sanguine developers. One of the early housing schemes, Clippers Quay, saw some of the most startling increases: the price of a two-bedroom flat, which when new in 1984 was available at the 'affordable' price of £39,495, more than tripled in two years, so that by 1986 it was £125,000, while a year later it had risen to £199,995.[47] The price of land similarly rose: in 1985 the Great Eastern Self-Build Housing Association was able to buy a riverside site of 1.4 acres at Maconochie's Wharf for a little over £250,000 an acre, in 1986 Ideal Homes paid over £1 million an acre for the 14.4-acre non-riverside Timber Wharves, while by May 1987 the cost of riverside land suitable for residential development was approaching £3 million per acre,[48] and a record £4 million an acre was paid for the prime Cumberland Mills site overlooking Greenwich.[49]

Such quick profits attracted considerable numbers of speculators, or 'dealers',[50] who added to the price-inflation. Usually such speculators would put down retainers on a number of dwellings, even before work began on site, expecting to sell them at a higher figure before they had to complete the original sale and pay the full price.[51] According to the *Financial Times* in December 1987, research showed that about 60 per cent of advance sales of new dwellings in Docklands had been to speculators.[52] As a result, little less than a mania was created,[53] which at its height saw second-hand flats on one development on the Island being offered at £35,000 more than a new one could be purchased for when bought direct from the developer.[54]

Difficult Times

During 1987 and 1988 several factors combined to depress the Docklands housing market. The crash on the Stock Market in October 1987, when the value of shares tumbled, slowed down house sales on the Isle of Dogs. By this time higher-priced properties, over £120,000, were becoming increasingly difficult to sell, and speculators were beginning to relinquish their options to buy unfinished dwellings.[55] Also, from the early 1970s onwards, the special attraction of Docklands had been the novelty of living in redundant warehouses, but by 1987 there were few of these left to convert.[56] Ironically, on the Isle of Dogs, the only conversion of old industrial premises into residential – at Burrell's Wharf – was then being launched.

The large number of new housing schemes which became available in Docklands during 1987 and 1988

28. The ambitious central axis of Timber Wharves Village, looking south along Ashdown Walk (see page 43).

aroused fears of a massive over-supply. To compound developers' problems, building costs were rising rapidly, by about 20 per cent a year, threatening the economic viability of those schemes under construction and deferring some which had not been started.[57] Simultaneously, in 1988, potential purchasers were discouraged when the double tax-relief on a single mortgage for a couple was withdrawn and interest rates were raised. As house prices dropped nationally, those in Docklands – just as they had risen more steeply than elsewhere – now began to fall more rapidly.[58] By late 1988, therefore, a number of developers were giving considerable price reductions, directly or indirectly, in an attempt to sell their properties,[59] and some owners re-selling flats overlooking the river on the Isle of Dogs had to accept prices between 4 and 16 per cent below those they had expected.[60]

House sales in the area continued to fall:[61] in 1988, 205 new dwellings had been sold in Docklands during one month, but throughout the first 7½ months of 1989 only 300 were sold, out of more than 2,000 available.[62] Strangled by slow sales, high interest rates, and escalating building costs, the Kentish Property Group found itself in trouble with its Burrell's Wharf development, and in July 1989 went into receivership.[63] The psychological effect of this was far reaching, and dramatically altered the popular perception of Docklands.[64] There had previously been some criticisms, but they now became more widespread, and began to come from the least likely sources. Very soon after the Kentish crash, a director of a leading merchant bank expressed the fear that 'the risk and nightmare is that a ghost city is being created down in docklands, an environment where people will not want to live and work'. Even the chief executive of another house-building company involved in developments on the Isle of Dogs complained that the Island was one great building site and hardly seemed the ideal place to live.[65] Until then the difficulties had seemed only temporary, now it seemed that they might prove terminal.

As the seller's market changed to a buyer's one, so developers had to resort to greater incentives in an attempt to sell new properties. This process can be traced particularly well at Cyclops Wharf, where in the second half of 1988 Fairclough Homes offered purchasers £1,000 a month for a year, to cover payments on the first year's mortgage.[66] In the following year they introduced an equity participation scheme whereby not only was 10 per cent of the purchase price deferred, but the mortgage was subsidised by fixing the interest rate at 10.5 per cent for the first two years. Even so, by January 1990, only 39 of the 200 flats had been sold in almost two years, and so a 'Fair Share' scheme was introduced whereby buyers paid 50 per cent of the asking price at the outset and the remainder at any time during the next five years at the then market value.[67] A few months later, in May 1990, on top

29. Old and New at Burrell's Wharf: the converted 1850s Plate House *(centre)* is flanked by two new ranges, Beacon House *(right)* and Slipway House. View looking north-west across the 'square' (see page 32).

30. Cyclops Wharf, a development completed in 1990, offering a range of accommodation from studio apartments to four-bedroom houses (see page 37).

of the 50-per-cent scheme, Fairclough also offered mortgages at 7.5 per cent (half the normal interest rate at the time) for 18 months.[68] Apartments in this development were still being advertised, with various inducements, in July 1992.[69]

In their desperation, developers turned to other expedients. On the Cumberland Mills development, *Building Design* reported in September 1989 that two half-completed blocks were being sealed without internal fixtures and fittings.[70] At Timber Wharves, where only 37 dwellings had been sold to private buyers, Ideal Homes preferred to offer them their money back, and sell all the other 421 new homes to the LDDC, which paid £65 million in 1989 so that it could rehouse council tenants displaced by the Limehouse Link road.[71] In 1992 the LDDC sold some of the dwellings at Timber Wharves to three housing associations for letting to council tenants who wanted a move.[72] In 1991, 40 flats at The Anchorage were let to Tower Hamlets Council to provide housing for teachers.[73]

As house sales dwindled, so the number of residential properties available for rent increased. In the autumn of 1989, for example, one- and two-bedroom flats at Clippers Quay were offered at rents of between £125 and £135 per week.[74] New legislation in that year increased the attractiveness of renting out properties by enabling landlords to charge market rents and introducing 'assured shorthold' tenancies for a minimum of six months (with a new contract after the agreed period).[75]

By October 1990 construction of new dwellings for sale in Docklands had virtually ceased, with about 1,500 completed dwellings still unsold, and it was estimated that the existing rate of sales would have to increase by 50 per cent to clear this over-supply by the end of 1991.[76] Among the sites where plans for residential developments have been drawn up and agreed, but had not been implemented by May 1995, are Clyde & Langbourne Wharves, Cubitt Town Wharf, Ferguson's Wharf, Hutching's Wharf, Millwall Wharf, Ocean Wharf and Winkley's Wharf – the majority being riverside sites on the west side of the Island. At Glengall Bridge West, a block intended as housing was remodelled as 'Business Apartments', complete with kitchens and bathrooms, while at Timber Wharves show houses and flats were demolished in 1991, to make way for a proposed office block.[77]

At the same time, the financial position of the LDDC forced it, at the Government's request, to review its social housing strategy and to cut its 1990–4 new-build programme to 19 per cent of its housing budget, compared with the 72 per cent envisaged in its 1989 strategy, the remainder being allocated for the refurbishment of existing buildings. Overall, the social housing programme for the period was cut by more than half, from £49 million to £21.9 million.[78] In April 1991 Eric Sorenson, the newly appointed Chief Executive of the LDDC, after pointing out that Urban Development Corporations (UDCs) were set up 'as temporary or short-life organizations with a remit to promote development as fast as reasonably possible', stated that 'it is not consistent with that objective to also require UDCs to engage in a wide range of investment and social provision programmes'.[79]

Equilibrium?

In 1989–90 the future of the residential developments on the Isle of Dogs, as much as the commercial ones, was thought to be dependent on the success or otherwise of Canary Wharf.[80] Yet, despite the fact that Canary Wharf went into administration in May 1992, there were already some signs of a revival in the housing market in Docklands.[81] House sales began to pick up during the first half of 1991 and continued in 1992, although, at Cumberland Mills, at least, this was only achieved by dropping prices in 1991 by as much as 40 per cent and arranging low-interest mortgages.[82] This upturn encouraged developers to resume the construction of new housing, with the commencement of another 120 dwellings at Burrell's Wharf in 1992 and more than 100 low-cost starter homes at Timber Wharves in 1993,[83] and at least a further four schemes in 1994–5. Several of the latest developments, including that at Timber Wharves, are, however, in stark contrast to the luxurious Docklands apartments of the 1980s and mark something of a return to 'affordable' homes. In contrast to national trends, sales of new homes in Docklands have risen quite dramatically, with over 1,400 sold in 1994, representing an increase of 163 per cent on 1993.[84]

Undoubtedly, several developers were caught out by the sudden slump in the housing market and suffered serious financial damage as a result. Similarly, those buyers who purchased dwellings at the height of the boom saw the value of their properties drastically eroded.

31. Cumberland Mills, south-east apartment block, overlooking the former Newcastle drawdock (see page 37).

However, the *Independent* concluded in May 1992 that in Docklands:

Prices have fallen more than 30 per cent since the boom – but that is no worse than elsewhere in London. People who paid as little as £50,000 for a flat and £110,000 for a four-bedroomed house on the Isle of Dogs in 1985 are still ahead of the game.[85]

An article written early in 1995 on housing property on the Isle of Dogs suggested the following purchase prices as an approximate guide: '£45–50,000 for a small studio flat, £52–62,000 for a one-bed apartment, £80–100,000 for a reasonable two-bed flat, and from £82,000 for a decent three-bed family house'.[86]

Gazetteer of Housing Developments

The numbers in the margins identify the location of the developments as shown on the plan on page 21.

2 *Ambassador Square*

This consists of 31 dwellings on the site of George W. Mancell's steel yard, at the north-eastern end of Cahir Street (*22*). It is a mixture of one- and two-bedroom flats and three-bedroom houses, arranged around a central, enclosed courtyard, developed and constructed by Laing Homes in 1988 using its own standard housing-types.[87]

3 *The Anchorage*

This development, to the west of Westferry Road, stands on the southern part of Sufferance Wharf, where Beechams had a soft-drinks depot (*24, 61*). It was developed by Rosehaugh Copartnership Developments, the architects were Michael Squire Associates, and the main contractor was Costain Management Design of Maidenhead. One ten-storey and two four-storey blocks, completed in 1990, provide 120 apartments, nine terraced houses, a leisure centre, and four commercial units.[88]

5 *Bristow/Cairns Triangle, Glengall Grove*

This residential development on a triangular site at the junction of Glengall Grove and East Ferry Road will consist of 38 one-bedroom and 15 two-bedroom flats (together with one shop unit) in a two- to four-storey block. Designed by Michael Ginn Associates for Galliard Homes, construction was under way in May 1995.[89]

6 *Burrell's Wharf*

Of all the residential developments projected on the Isle of Dogs in the 1980s, Kentish Homes' Burrell's Wharf was, for several reasons, one of the most remarkable. The site was the richest in terms of historical association, covering part of the site of Napier Yard, on which Isambard Kingdom Brunel's *Great Eastern* was built in the 1850s.

The development was also unique in the extent to which it involved the retention of old buildings and in its preservation of an intricate, organic pattern of building. It was notable, too, for the diversity of its architectural forms and its intended range of uses in addition to housing. Stylistically, it eschewed Post-Modernism in favour of a robust post-industrial vernacular: 'dockland in Docklands', as Kentish put it (*29*).[90]

Kentish was controlled by Keith Preston and his wife Kay, who had taken over the house-builders Kentish Homes in 1985. A surveyor by training, Preston described himself as 'really a frustrated architect'.[91] From refurbishing terraced houses, the Prestons went on to carry out a series of increasingly ambitious schemes, all in East London, from the modest conversion into flats of Bowbrook School in Bow, to Cascades (see page 34).

In July 1987 Kentish Property Group plc was floated, achieving a peak share price in October that year, just before the stock market crash on 'Black Monday'. Undeterred, Kentish pressed on with Burrell's Wharf. After a rise in interest rates had badly affected the housing market, sales at Burrell's Wharf ceased, and in July 1989 Kentish sought suspension from the stock market. The Halifax Building Society, which had loaned £25 million for Burrell's Wharf, thereupon appointed a receiver to the development. Simultaneously, Security Pacific, which had financed Kentish's Bow Quarter, called in receivers to that development. By the end of July Kentish was in receivership. J. A. Elliott, the main contractors for both Burrell's Wharf and Bow Quarter, later went into administrative receivership. The partly completed development, somewhat modified, was relaunched by Halifax New Homes Services in 1992.

Designed by Jestico & Whiles, the Burrell's Wharf scheme, when completed, will comprise seven large residential buildings, with a mixture of smaller shop, office and residential premises fronting Westferry Road. On the north side of the site, twin ranges erected in 1907–8 for Venesta Ltd, the plywood manufacturers, and later absorbed into Burrell's colour works, have been converted into 93 apartments, called Slipway House. This conversion was intended to convey, through exposed beams and brickwork, the sought-after 'warehouse' atmosphere.

Beacon House, built around the stump of the chimney of the Millwall Iron Works shipyard, and a smaller block behind it, Port House, are new buildings designed to have the same 'warehouse' feel. Both have reinforced-concrete frames with brick cladding. At the riverside are two new nine-storey blocks, Chart House and Deck House (formerly Bridge and Wheelhouse), each comprising 70 apartments (*32*). Here, 'designer sophistication' was aimed at, rather than warehouse ruggedness. Both blocks are of reinforced-concrete framing clad externally with concrete panels.

At the centre of the development, the Plate House – erected by Cubitt & Company in the 1850s for John Scott Russell, the builder of the *Great Eastern* – was intended to contain, in addition to 19 small apartments and a penthouse in the tower, the 'Island Club' complex, comprising

32. Deck House *(left)* and Chart House, apartment blocks at Burrell's Wharf: looking south-east towards Greenwich.

swimming pool and gymnasium, sauna and sunbed, function room and wine bar. Finally, the 'Plate House Gallery' promised work and display space for residential artists, craftsmen and designers. On Westferry Road, the Quarters, a new building with a distinctive corner rotunda, was to contain 21 shop and business units, and 16 split-level apartments above. The former warehouse and offices beside the entrance to the wharf, renamed the Gatehouse, is to be refurbished to provide three floors of offices. Between it and the former Robert Burns public house, the ground was cleared to provide a new entrance to the Plate House. Nos 264–266 Westferry Road are to be remodelled as Gantry House and Mast House, both comprising offices. Behind them, Loft House, formerly a warehouse and first-floor pattern room, has been refurbished, also for use as offices.

Caledonian Wharf

This housing scheme stands on a riverside site east of Saunders Ness Road, and includes Caledonian Wharf Road and Storers Way. The four-acre site was developed and built by Thomas Bates & Son of Coventry and Romford in 1984–7, with a scheme designed by Alan Turner & Associates. There are 100 houses and flats; the flats are arranged along the riverside in a continuous

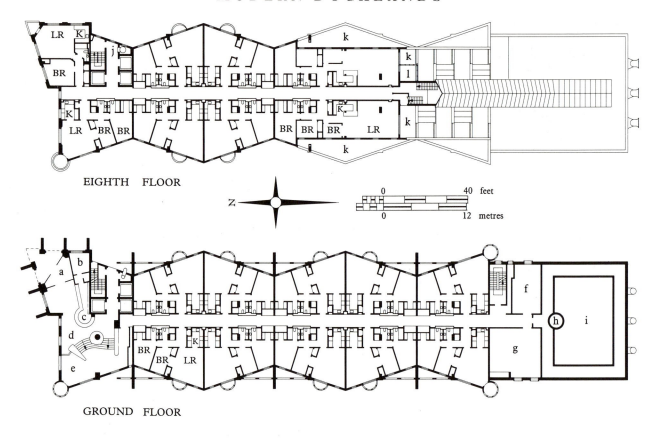

EIGHTH FLOOR

z

| 0 | | 40 | feet |
| 0 | | 12 | metres |

GROUND FLOOR

33. Cascades apartment block, ground- and eighth-floor plans.
Key: a Main Entrance: b Porter's Office: c Reception Desk: d Foyer: e Quiet Sitting Area: f Cleaner's Store:
g Conference Room: h Spa: i Swimming Pool: j Refuse Chute: k Roof Terrace: l Conservatory

series of blocks, varying from two to five storeys (*21*); the houses range from two to four storeys, and are mainly arranged in a loose courtyard-fashion. The old dry dock on the site has been transformed into an ornamental lake.[92]

11 *Cascades*

The tall apartment block, known as Cascades, which overlooks the river, off Westferry Road, is already a distinctive local landmark (*Frontispiece, 61*). After Canary Wharf it is the best-known building on the Isle of Dogs, not least because it was criticized by the Prince of Wales and appears on the cover of his book, *A Vision of Britain* (1989). The northern part of Sufferance Wharf, on which Cascades is situated, was purchased, with planning permission for three- and four-storey houses, in 1985 by Kentish Homes. However, the architects, Campbell, Zogolovitch, Wilkinson & Gough, who had already designed a number of low-rise housing schemes for Kentish Homes, looked at other waterside developments in such cities as Sydney and San Francisco, and decided that this site demanded a tall building. The developer and the LDDC were therefore persuaded to accept a 20-storey block of apartments designed by one of the partners, Rex

Wilkinson – a return to the high-rise housing which had gone out of favour in the 1960s.

Construction was by J. A. Elliott (the contract being provisionally costed at £14.8 million), using fast-track methods (*23*). The first occupant had moved in by February 1988, and the scheme was completed in August, only a little over the 18 months originally demanded.

The main block is clad with brick, principally buff and blue, although some yellow stocks are also used (*34*). It contains 164 one- to three-bedroom flats on either side of central corridors. The building gradually reduces in size as it gets higher and the side walls are concertina-shaped on plan (*33*). All this is designed to give each flat the best orientation. The south-facing slope of the building provides a 'cascade' of sun terraces and alternating greenhouses for the penthouses, and also incorporates the fire escape under a steel-and-glass canopy. The deliberately nautical style (which the architects had already employed at New Concordia Wharf in Bermondsey), uses portholes, railings and 'bird's nest' balconies to convey the streamlined qualities of an ocean liner. The block also has a leisure centre, with swimming pool and gymnasium. A lower block of three and four storeys is set at right angles to the main block and contains four shops, with apartments above.[93]

34. Cascades apartment block, the riverside front looking north.

13 *Clippers Quay*

This comprises 258 flats and houses built around the former graving dock, at the south-east corner of the Millwall
Docks, on land owned by the Port of London Authority,
which shared in the development profits (*18, 26*). The
scheme, which won design awards, was drawn up by
Robert Martin Associates, and was developed and built
by Roger Malcolm Ltd in 1984–8, at an estimated cost of
£11 million. Access off Spindrift Avenue to Clippers
Quay is provided by Undine Road and Whiteadder Way,
and the development also includes Falcon Way.[94]

14 *Compass Point*

The Compass Point development, straddling the north-
ern end of Saunders Ness Road, comprises Blyth Close,
Chichester Way, Mariners Mews, Sextant Avenue, and
Francis Close, and stands on the site of Dudgeon's
Wharf. It was developed and constructed by Costain
Homes in 1985–8, using a scheme initially drawn up by
Jeremy Dixon of Jeremy Dixon-Building Design Partnership. Dixon's aim, both in the overall layout and the design of the individual groups of buildings at Compass
Point, was to re-create the urban pattern of Georgian
London 'in which formality and axiality are tempered by
asymmetry and modesty of elevation'. The intention was
to design in the Classical spirit, rather than simply to
produce a neo-Georgian pastiche. There are 150 flats and
houses in a variety of blocks, faced in dark-red brick and
smooth white render, with pitched slate roofs. Several
blocks are re-workings of previous schemes by Dixon,
such as the three-storey villas in Sextant Avenue (based
on his Lanark Road housing at Maida Vale), the Dutch-
style riverside terrace with stepped gables (derived from
his St Mark's Road housing, Kensington), and the terraces with tall triangular windows in Chichester Way
(adapted from his Ashmill Street scheme, Paddington)
(*36*). Sextant Avenue also provides the main axial vista,
with – at one end – a small terraced, somewhat Regency-
style crescent, and – at the other end – a view of silos

35. Compass Point, looking east along Sextant Avenue.

36. Compass Point, looking east along Chichester Way.

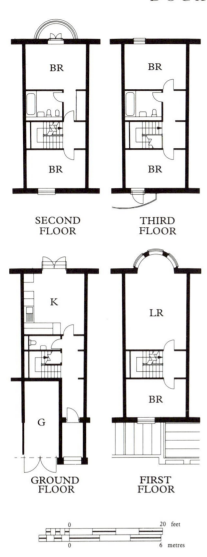

SECOND   THIRD
FLOOR   FLOOR

GROUND   FIRST
FLOOR   FLOOR

37. Compass Point, plans of a typical four/five bedroom house
in Mariners Mews.

across the river, framed and echoed by two tall riverside
blocks of flats with full-height cylindrical towers (*25, 35*).
Beyond is a riverside walk, complete with pergolas.[95]

15 *Cumberland Mills*

Occupying the site of a Victorian seed-crushing works on
the south-east side of Saunders Ness Road, Cumberland
Mills was developed and built by Thomas Bates & Son in
two phases, completed in 1988 and 1990 (*31, 38*). The designer was a former GLC architect, Donald Ball, of Alan
Turner & Associates. There are 88 dwellings in all,
arranged in cluster-blocks rising to ten storeys, each clus-
ter being made up of a complex interlocking spiral of
one- to three-bedroom flats, arranged so that each flat has
its own terrace-garden overlooking the river. The design
is based on the GLC's award-winning Odhams housing
in Covent Garden, for which Ball was also responsible.[96]

Cyclops Wharf   16

This is a housing development to the west of Westferry
Road on the riverside site of the Le Bas Tubes foundry
(*30*). 'Cyclops' was the existing name of the site, an
allusion to the race of giant foundry workers of Classical
mythology. The development was a joint venture between
Abbey National Homes and Fairclough Homes. It was
designed by the Mason Richards Partnership of Dudley,
Worcestershire, and the main contractors were
Fairclough Building Ltd. The first block was finished
at the beginning of 1989, and the whole scheme was
completed in 1990. There are 200 dwellings, comprising
studio and one- to three-bedroom apartments, and three-
and four-bedroom houses, in blocks varying between four
and eleven storeys. The scheme also includes a swimming
pool, sauna, and gymnasium for residents, a ground-floor
car park set below the riverside block, and a double shop-
unit on the corner of Westferry Road.[97]

De Bruin Court, Nos 17–31 (odd) Ferry Street   17

This is a small development by Moram Homes Ltd, and
the scheme was completed in 1988 (*39*). No. 17 is a four-
storey block with seven flats, Nos 19–29 are five three-
storey and one four-storey (No. 29) terraced houses, and
No. 31 is a three-storey detached house. Stylistically they

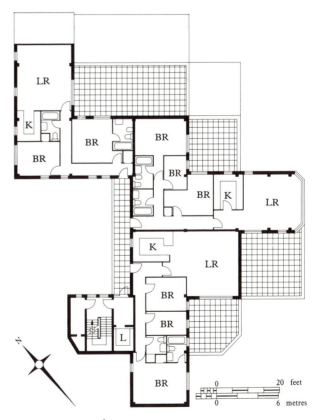

38. Cumberland Mills, south-west apartment block, second-
floor plan.

39. De Bruin Court, Nos 17-31 (odd) Ferry Street.

are a mixture of metropolitan Georgian and seaside Regency, with a touch of 'Docklands nautical'.[98]

18   Dockers Tanner Road Scheme

This four-storey block of apartments, designed by BUJ (Barnard Urquhart Jarvis) Partnership for Whitechapel Land Ltd, was under construction in May 1995.[99]

22   Felstead Gardens

Standing off Ferry Street and on the site of Felsted [*sic*] Wharf, this is a small housing scheme of 28 flats and 10 town houses, in three- and four-storey blocks, developed and built in 1983–5 by Wates Built Homes, and designed by Wigley Fox. This scheme received a Department of the Environment Housing Design Award in 1985.[100]

24   Friars Mead

Except for Nos 105 and 107, which are part of Glengall Self-Build (see below), Friars Mead was built as a result of a limited design competition organized by the LDDC. It was won by Comben Homes Ltd (subsequently taken over by the Trafalgar House Group's Ideal Homes company), with a scheme designed by Ronald Quinn Associates. Work began in 1983, but because of the low-lying nature of the site, at the north-east corner of

the Mudchute, which required special drainage work, and problems caused by the toxicity of the soil, the scheme was not completed until 1986.

This development consists of 24 one-bedroom flats, and 48 two- and three-bedroom houses. Taking its lead from the Development Corporation's brief, which mentioned 'quad' housing, a number of dwellings at the centre of the scheme are built in such blocks. Each contains four dwellings and has a slightly Japanese-pagoda appearance.[101]

Gallions View   25

Located at the northern end of Stewart Street, on the east side, this £6.25 million development of 67 one- and two-bedroom flats in a five- and six-storey block, designed by Lawrence & Wrightson, was begun by Barratts London Ltd in 1995. It is due for completion in mid-1996.[102]

Glengall Bridge

See below, page 71.

Glengall Place   27

This housing scheme consists of Nos 20–74 (even) Tiller Road (on the south side), plus Claire Place. The 79 traditional one- to three-bedroom, two-storey houses were jointly developed by Barratt (East London) and the Boleyn and Forest Housing Society for shared-ownership occupancy, and were built by Barratts in 1984–5, using its own standard house-types.[103]

Glengall Self-Build   28

This development consists of Nos 1–8 (consec) Isambard Close, Nos 1–6 (consec) St James Close and Nos 105 and 107 Friars Mead (*40*). The scheme, by the Glengall Self-Build Housing Association, varies from the other two self-build schemes in the area, at Maconochie's Wharf and Arcadia Street, in that it was initiated and organized by a firm of professional advisers, the Essex Self-Build Advisory Service, based at Pitsea. The firm arranged the purchase of the 1.1-acre site from the LDDC (which provided the infrastructure), obtained 100-per-cent funding from the Housing Corporation, commissioned Saunders and Huggins of Greys, Essex, to draw up plans (project architect Roy Bromage), sought people to form an association and provided the constitution for it, arranged the purchase of materials, and co-ordinated and supervised work on site. The 16 members of the association, who were all local people, carried out the work themselves, doing about 26 hours a week. The project started in September 1985, the houses were completed by the summer of 1987, and were handed over to individual members in December of that year. For an outlay of £32,500 each member obtained a three-bedroom house valued at between £90,000 and £110,000. The consultants received

40. Glengall Self-Build Housing Scheme, looking north-east from the Mudchute towards London Yard and *(left)* Kelson House.

a percentage of the development costs, drawn from each member's contribution.

These two-storey houses are designed to blend in with the adjacent housing in Friars Mead by Comben Homes, and adopt a similar 'pavilion' form. The main differences are that the self-build houses are semi-detached, rather than in groups of four, and have square-fronted, double-storey bay windows.[104]

35 ## *Horseshoe Court*

This lies between Manchester Road and Ferry Street. It is a further development by Wates Built Homes, following the immediate success of their nearby Felstead Gardens. The architects were again Wigley Fox, and Wates acted as its own main contractor, with work being carried out in 1987–8. The name of this development is derived from the United Horse Shoe & Nail Company which manufactured horseshoes in Ferry Street between 1881 and 1907. The accommodation was aimed particu-

larly at first-time buyers with young children. The 71 one- and two-bedroom flats are mainly arranged in two-, three- and four-storey blocks around an inner courtyard. There are nine three-bedroom houses arranged in two two-storey terraces facing Manchester Road (Nos 64–80, even). The remaining flats are to the west, in a separate L-shaped three-storey block on the corner of Ferry Street and Manchester Road.[105]

Jamestown Harbour 39

This development extends round the east and south sides of the Blackwall Basin, either side of the basin entrance, and continues around the former West India Dock Graving Dock. It is also planned to be extended to the east of Preston's Road. In 1982 the PLA, which owned most of the 6.8-acre site, invited Wates Built Homes to develop this site and the housing scheme was designed by Whittam, Cox, Clayton & Ellis. Construction was carried out by Wates itself in phases: Bridge House Quay (also

41. Jamestown Harbour: Cotton's Landing from the south-east. In the foreground is Franta Belsky's sculpture 'Leap'.

including Landons Close), 1984–6; Virginia Moorings (around Lancaster Close), completed in 1986; Cotton's Landing (named after Joseph Cotton, the first chairman of the East India Dock Company, and approached from Preston's Road via Lovegrove Walk), 1988–early 1990s. When the Cotton's Landing phase is complete, there will be 210 dwellings on this development, providing one- to three-bedroom apartments, and four-bedroom houses (*27*). A sculpture by Franta Belsky of eight dolphins spouting water, entitled 'Leap', was commissioned by Wates for the former graving dock (*41*).[106]

40 ### La Caye Housing Scheme

This development is situated on the south-west corner of Manchester Road and Glenaffric Avenue. It was designed by Levitt Bernstein Associates Ltd for La Caye Housing Co-op Ltd and built by Kingsbury Construction in 1993–4. A four-storey block of eight two-bedroom flats stands on the corner of the two streets, while a terrace of six three-storey houses runs along Glenaffric Avenue. Both blocks are faced in banded brick and the hipped roofs are covered in concrete tiles.[107]

44 ### Lockes Field

This lies between Chapel House Street and Westferry Road. It was developed, designed, and built in 1988–9 by Groveside Homes, a subsidiary of Tarmac. A central 'mews', approached via an archway through the gatehouses at either end, lies between two enclosed court-

yards. There are 90 houses and flats in two- and three-storey blocks, faced in dark-red mottled brick and with pitched, slated roofs (*42, 43*).[108]

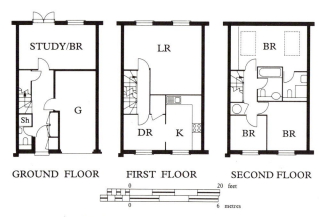

42. Lockes Field, plans of a typical four-bedroom house.

46 ### London Yard

The site of about ten acres, on the east side of Manchester Road, was developed by VOM (Vastgoed Ourwikkelings Maatschappi), a Dutch-based property development company (*8, 40*). The original scheme was drawn up by ED, a Dutch architectural practice, but its execution was supervised by the London-based Building Design Partnership. Construction was carried out in phases in 1984–8 by John Laing, at a reported cost of £11.5 million. London Yard embraces Amsterdam Road, Leerdam Drive, Rembrandt Close and Rotterdam Drive, and consists of 295 dwellings in a wide mixture of flats, maisonettes and houses. Six- and seven-storey apartment blocks line the riverside, while to their rear lower terraces of two, three and four storeys are built around gardens. At the centre of the scheme is a specially created lake, which is not only ornamental, but also helps to drain the site. The scheme includes a small parade of 14 shop units, a restaurant and a public riverside walk.[109]

47 ### Luralda Gardens

This development is on the site of the Luralda timber factory (which closed down in 1982) to the east of Island Gardens. It is a housing scheme developed, designed, and built in 1983–5, by Barratt (East London). There are 48 dwellings, arranged around three sides of a courtyard garden and there is a riverside terrace.[110]

49 ### Maconochie's Wharf

This housing scheme, on the south-west side of Westferry Road, in Maconochie's Road, Wynan Road, Pointers Close, Rainbow Avenue and Blasker Walk, is the result of three self-build projects, all designed by the same architects, Stout & Litchfield (project architect Roy Stout).[111]

43. Lockes Field, looking south.

The scheme was largely inspired by Dr Michael Barra-clough, who had already worked with these architects on a housing scheme in Ferry Street, of which only four houses were eventually built, and Jill Palios of Wapping. Both keen protagonists of self-build, they were also anxious to see some of the new housing going to local inhabitants. By leaflet distribution, advertising in local papers, and word of mouth, enough people were recruited to form the Great Eastern Self-Build Association in 1985.[112] Maconochie's Wharf had been intended for light industrial purposes, but the LDDC, which owned it and had carried out reclamation work there, was persuaded to sell 1.4 acres (with the infrastructure) at the District Valuer's price of £364,000 – remarkably cheap in the light of subsequent land prices in the area.[113]

Because the Great Eastern Association had 46 members rather than the 20 recommended for such associations by the Housing Corporation, difficulties were encountered raising a loan. The Abbey National Building Society eventually provided the finance, the total cost of this part of the scheme being estimated at £1.7 million.[114] The Association commissioned Stout & Litchfield to design the housing. As about a half of the members were in the building trades, a traditional brick-construction method could be used, rather than one more specifically designed for self-build. The members wanted houses, and terraced housing seemed the only way of using the site economically and without appearing to overcrowd it. The LDDC insisted that the river frontage should be uniform, each dwelling being of the same height, with identical balconies, windows, and chimneys. Otherwise there are slight variations in external features, such as the fenestration (including, in some cases, the addition of a bay window), the provision of stained wooden balconies, and the number of storeys, ranging from two- to three-storeys-and-attics (*44*). The dwellings are generally gabled but, again, for variety these are given different dispositions. Also, the internal planning was agreed after owners had first filled in a questionnaire which indicated the possible options available and then had a personal interview with

44. Maconochie's Wharf Self-Build Housing Scheme: Blasker Walk looking north-east into Pointers Close.

the architects. Thus, while each owner had some opportunity to incorporate preferences, the architects were able to impose an overall unity, which restricted any wild eccentricities and prevented visual anarchy. The use of the same building materials throughout the whole development also contributes to the overall unity: white calcium silicate bricks (but see below), slates on pitched roofs, and hardwood windows.

Construction of the Great Eastern project (most of the houses on the southern half of the site) began in June 1986.[115] A certain amount of work was contracted out, mainly the piled foundations and the roof-slating. A member of the association was paid as a full-time site manager, but otherwise members had to devote a minimum of 20 hours a week of their spare time, usually at weekends, working communally on the project, and there were stiff fines for those who failed to turn up or were late.[116] Curiously, women were excluded from working on the site. The first houses were completed towards the end of 1987,[117] and in 1988 this scheme won a Prince of Wales's Community Enterprise Award.[118]

Sufficient interested people remained after the first project to form the nucleus for the second scheme: the Isle of Dogs Self-Build Housing Association. This association, with 35 members, was able to purchase the adjacent part of Maconochie's Wharf, to the north of the Great Eastern scheme, from the LDDC in 1987, although the (undisclosed) price, again fixed by the District Valuer,

was much higher than for the first scheme.[119] Work began about the middle of that year and the actual building work took only 19 months (six months ahead of schedule), with the first houses occupied by February 1989.[120] However, construction was speeded up by contracting out more of the work than on the other schemes, it being more economic to do so because of the level of interest rates at the time. The terraces are similar to the Great Eastern ones, but those abutting the Burrell's Wharf site were required by the LDDC to be faced in yellow brick instead of white, to match the development there.

Finally, the eight houses ranged in two terraces to either side of the Ship public house in Westferry Road were built by the Second Isle of Dogs Self-Build Housing Association. Planning permission was granted in August 1988 and a licence was issued to allow initial piling work to start prior to formal purchase. In this case the LDDC allowed the purchase of the land to be paid for in instalments and when the houses were complete the owners had the option of either paying the outstanding 50 per cent of the land value or entering into an equity-share arrangement with the Corporation.[121] These houses, completed towards the end of 1990, are faced in yellow brick. Rainbow Avenue and Wynan Road are named after ships which regularly berthed at Maconochie's Wharf, while Blasker Walk commemorates a local doctor.[122]

In all there are 89 three-bedroom houses, which cost less than £30,000 each to build, while the overall cost per dwelling, including the price of the land, was less than £50,000.[123] If members of the associations sold their houses within five years of completion they had to pay back a proportion of any profits.[124]

52 Masthouse Terrace

This group of public housing, off Westferry Road, was developed by the East London Housing Association in the early 1990s. The site was acquired by the LDDC from Tower Hamlets Borough Council in 1981, but in 1983 part of it was transferred back to the Council in return for land which it owned in Royal Mint Street.[125] Clearance and filling was carried out by the LDDC during 1984, at a cost of £790,000,[126] but Tower Hamlets had difficulty in obtaining the finance to build dwellings there.[127] Negotiations took place in 1987–8 between the LDDC, the Borough Council, and various other parties over a joint development on 8.6 acres of land, of which 3 acres were owned by the Council and 5.6 by the LDDC. It was proposed that these two authorities, in association with Countryside Developments, the Abbey National Building Society, and the East London Housing Association, would build properties for sale on some of the LDDC's land. The money raised was to be used to finance the construction of 171 dwellings, for rent through the Housing Association, on a site partly owned by Tower Hamlets and partly by the Corporation. The Council was to have the right of nomination to all of the homes.[128]

The collapse in the housing market on the Isle of Dogs meant that building houses for sale was no longer a viable proposition. Eventually, in March 1990, it was announced that 175 homes were to be developed by the East London Housing Association on four acres of the Masthouse Terrace site. The scheme cost £21.5 million. This included land from the Council valued at £2.9 million and grants of £7.2 million from the LDDC and £8 million from the Housing Corporation.

The scheme was designed by the Alan J. Smith Partnership and construction was by Countryside Homes (1990–2).[129] The blocks are in yellow brick, with bands of blue brick, and have slated, pitched roofs. Beside the river, the six-storey Phoenix Court has some nautical touches (19), as does the adjacent three-storey block in Masthouse Terrace. The rest of the dwellings are arranged in two- and three-storey blocks on either side of Britannia Road and in courtyard fashion around Vulcan Square and Cutlers Square. The accommodation ranges from one-bedroom flats to six-bedroom houses, and there is also provision for 16 elderly people, as well as two Health Authority 'Care in the Community' units. Tower Hamlets Borough Council has 50 per cent of the nomination rights to dwellings.[130]

60 Omega Close

This scheme, at the east end of Tiller Road, on the south side, was designed by ECD Architects for the East London Housing Association. It was built in 1994–5 by Countryside Homes and consists of a six-bedroom and nine three-bedroom houses, and six one-bedroom flats, in two red-brick, three-storey blocks with tiled roofs.[131]

63 Plymouth Wharf

This housing scheme, off the east side of Saunders Ness Road, consists of 62 dwellings. It was developed, designed and built by Groveside Homes, and was completed early in 1986. Three-storey terraces to either side of an inner courtyard lead down to a pair of warehouse-style blocks (also of three storeys) by the riverside.[132]

65 Potter's Lodge, Nos 14–28 (even) Manchester Road

This development was instigated by Lee Savell (New Cross) Ltd, but was sold on to Furlong Homes. It consists of 12 two-bedroom flats in a four-storey block, faced in yellow brick with red brick dressings and roofed in artificial slate. The scheme was designed by the 20/4 Partnership and was under construction in March 1995.[133]

68 Quay West

Quay West lies to the east of Westferry Road, and includes the west end of Spindrift Avenue, as well as Barnfield Place and Ironmongers Place. It was developed, designed, and built in 1988–9 by Wimpey Homes. There are 89 houses and 38 flats which provide one- to four-bedroom accommodation. The three- and four-storey blocks are arranged around two principal enclosures – 'a paragon and a pleasance', according to the developers' sales brochure.[134]

74 Thames Circle

This development, designed by Bradgate Homes for Galliard Homes Ltd, is situated on the site of Nos 269–285 (odd) Westferry Road, on the east side of the road. It is adjacent to Timber Wharves Village, which it resembles in style. There are 13 two-bedroom and three three-bedroom terraced houses, together with 18 one-bedroom flats, all brick-faced and two storeys in height. The development was completed in 1995.[135]

77 Timber Wharves Village

This is on a 14.4-acre site, at the western end of the south side of the Millwall Docks, just to the east of Westferry Road. The first part, designed by Barnard Urquhart Jarvis, and developed and constructed by Ideal Homes (part of the Trafalgar House Group), was built in phases between 1987 and 1992. The scheme has a strong urban character, with a fairly formal street layout (45). A central axis, Ashdown Walk, is closed by a large, curved six- and seven-storey block at the southern end with a central archway (28). The development is intended to consist of

45. Timber Wharves Village, looking north down Dartmoor Walk.

485 dwellings (in a wide mixture of flats and houses, with blocks varying, to date, between two and seven storeys), and to embrace also Arden Crescent, Barnsdale Avenue, Charnwood Gardens, Copeland Drive, Dartmoor Walk, Epping Close, Inglewood Close, Kintal Drive (renamed Dockers Tanner Road in 1990, as a reminder of the Great Dock Strike of 1889), Radnor Walk, Rothesay Walk, Savernake Close and Sherwood Gardens.[136] A second part, known as Corn Mill Quay, was designed and built by Fairview New Homes Plc in 1993–5. There are 113 dwellings arranged in studio, one- and two-bedroom flats, and three-bedroom town houses.

78   *Transom Square*

Transom Square, on the east side of Westferry Road, was developed, designed and built by Laing Homes. The three central blocks, of two and three storeys, comprising

31 one-bedroom flats and two-bedroom houses (less than half of the 64 dwellings planned for this site) were built between 1988 and 1990.[137]

No. 223 Westferry Road   81

This development on the south-west corner of Westferry Road and Tiller Road, designed by Hastingwood for the East London Housing Association and its subsidiary the Boleyn and Forest Housing Society Ltd, was built in 1994–5 by Tentford. It consists of 45 one- and two-bedroom flats and five three-bedroom houses in a U-shaped three- and four-storey block faced in pale brown brick, with an artificial slate roof. The block is arranged around an inner courtyard approached via a semi-circular-headed archway off Tiller Road. This site had been intended for commercial development as an extension to Tiller Court (see page 85).[138]

CHAPTER IV
Commercial Developments

Early Days

Before the LDDC's inception, the local authorities had made efforts to attract new firms to the Isle of Dogs and Docklands. They had some success: the City Corporation relocated the Billingsgate fish market on the north quay of the West India Docks (*46*), and Associated Dairies (ASDA) were persuaded to build a much-needed superstore on the Mudchute.[1]

The LDDC did, therefore, have a basis upon which to work. Initially, it sought to attract new firms involved in high-technology industries and services, such as computing, electronic and micro engineering, design and marketing services, and printing.[2] In fact, the earliest developments were relatively small-scale, courtyard-style business units on the pattern set by the Port of London Authority's Cannon Workshops (1982–3), or, following the example of the new Billingsgate Market (1980–1), high-tech 'shiny sheds'. The Lanterns (1983–4) (*47*), Indescon Court (1982–3) and Skylines (1985–6) are all courtyard-type schemes, while Milltech (completed in 1984), the PDX and Ladkarn Buildings (both completed in 1985), and Advance House (completed in 1987) are examples of 'shiny sheds'. Generally speaking, these buildings were typical of those on contemporary business parks being built all over the country. However, *Design* magazine pointed out that there was a rather greater 'pro-

47. The Lanterns (Lanterns Court), Millharbour, built in 1983–4, was one of several early courtyard-type commercial developments (see page 78).

fusion of exterior detailing' than normal. It suggested that one reason for this was the LDDC's wish for new buildings which caught the attention and could attract further development.[3] Not only were such schemes small-scale, but they provided relatively few jobs. By February 1987 roughly 250 of the 300 new companies which had moved into the Isle of Dogs since 1982 had fewer than 13 employees.[4]

The Enterprise Zone

In order to encourage and speed up the development, the Government decided to designate much of the area centring on the West India and Millwall docks an Enterprise Zone (as provided for under the 1980 Local Government, Planning and Land Act), which provided substantial inducements for firms to move into Docklands. The zone, which was effective from April 1982, had its boundary carefully drawn to exclude developments already completed or in progress, such as Billingsgate Market (*17*).[5] The chief financial concessions were: freedom from local rates for a ten-year period until 1992, no development land tax, and 100-per-cent capital allowance for new commercial and industrial buildings, to be set against corporation and income taxes. In December 1986 the *Financial Times*, in announcing the proposed relocation of its printing works to Docklands, calculated that the £20,850,000 cost of the site and building would be reduced to £15,400,000 by the tax concessions offered in the Enterprise Zone.[6]

In addition, there were simplified planning procedures: the zone was set up with an overall planning scheme, and any proposed development that conformed to that scheme was deemed to have been given planning consent, unless it was considered a particularly sensitive

46. Entrance to Billingsgate Fish Market, West India Docks.

48. Development within the Enterprise Zone on the north-east side of Millwall Docks: Harbour Exchange is in the centre and the London Arena on the right.

site and therefore specifically excluded from the general planning provision.[7] Similarly, development within the zone was normally free of 'use class' planning controls, so that a structure originally intended to be a factory or warehouse could be converted to office use during the course of construction, without requiring further permission.[8] This relaxed attitude to planning was seen by some critics to produce an 'architectural zoo' or museum of self-contained exhibits where few parts seem to fit well together.[9] While such an attitude initially encouraged developers, it was eventually seen to be acting against their best interests. Brian Edwards argued that 'the buildings constructed to date run the risk of poor connections in terms of both public space and urban transport, and have little protection from unsuitable or unfriendly neighbours'.[10] Olympia & York, however, were quick to intercede with the LDDC over any planned schemes which seemed to threaten the setting at Canary Wharf.

Peter Hall was acknowledged by the Government as the originator of the idea of Enterprise Zones. He was one of the authors of the *New Society* article in 1969 (see page 9), and the Enterprise Zone concept owed much to the 'non-planning' philosophy advocated there, as well as Hall's subsequent 'Freeport solution' to the economic ills of inner cities, in which 'small, selected areas . . . would

be simply thrown open to all kinds of initiative, with minimal control'. In fact, in the latter case, he conceived much more freedom from legislation, including a complete absence of immigration controls, than the Government was prepared to countenance even in Enterprise Zones.[11]

'Wall Street on Water'

In September 1985 the *Financial Times* commented:

one of the last remaining areas in which docklands has yet to prove itself is in its ability to provide a feasible and attractive overflow location specifically for the City. Until recently, there have been virtually no signs that it was succeeding, either in encouraging institutions to fund City-oriented projects or in convincing traditional City occupiers to move to the docks.[12]

Nevertheless, 1985 and 1986 marked a watershed in the development of the Isle of Dogs, although the effects were not immediately evident. A number of factors combined to increase the attractiveness of the area as an alternative location for City-type offices, and to encourage investors to back such schemes.

The new attitude was signalled when, in the autumn of 1985, a consortium of North American investment banks

49. Wall Street on Water: from right to left, and in ascending order of size, South Quay Plaza 1, 2 and 3. In the background is the pyramid-capped tower of South Quay Waterside (see pages 82, 85).

announced plans for an office development of eight million sq.ft on Canary Wharf.[13] This, more than any other factor, engendered confidence in the investment potential of the area. Until that time most Docklands developments had been under 100,000 sq.ft, but the sheer scale of the proposals for Canary Wharf encouraged other developers to think in terms of much larger schemes.[14]

The second important factor was that from April 1986 Enterprise Zones became even more attractive to those companies and individuals seeking shelter from their tax liabilities. A general 75 per cent initial allowance against tax for investments in industrial buildings anywhere in the United Kingdom was abolished for expenditure incurred after 31 March 1986, except in Enterprise Zones. In November 1987 *Accountancy Age*, referring to Docklands, argued that 'there is little doubt that the capital allowances have been a hugely important factor in the developments to date', while an estate agent involved in letting commercial properties claimed in November 1989 that 'the justification for building vast amounts of space on the Isle of Dogs has not been occupant driven, but tax driven'.[15]

The third factor which helped to increase office development on the Isle of Dogs was the 'Big Bang' in the City in October 1986, when trading in stocks and shares was deregulated and new technology was introduced. As a result, new firms sprang up, existing ones were seeking to expand and were looking for more modern facilities. Moreover, as the *Financial Times* pointed out, 'the City of London, caught off balance by the speed of the revolution and determined to resist any development which threatens its architectural heritage, has so far been unwilling or unable to respond'.[16] Furthermore, in October 1985 the Bank of England announced that banking firms were no longer required to remain within the City's square mile.[17]

Quite rapidly, therefore, the Enterprise Zone became regarded as an alternative to the City as a suitable venue for offices. Already in the summer of 1986 Norman Tebbit, then Secretary of State for Trade and Industry, was predicting that the West India and Millwall Docks might become 'Manhattan-on-Thames' or a 'Wall Street on water'.[18] By December of that year just over 14.6 million sq.ft of actual or potential office space had either been built or was planned on the Isle of Dogs, most of it within the Enterprise Zone.[19]

The effect of all this was, firstly, that low-rise developments in the course of construction, such as Great Eastern Enterprise, which were envisaged as a mixture of light-industrial and office use, became entirely offices,[20] and secondly, plans for unbuilt phases of existing developments were quickly revised. At Great Eastern Enterprise the final two phases, begun in 1987 and completed in 1989, consist of two office blocks of five and six storeys, in contrast to the two-storey units of the first phase. At Heron Quays, a near neighbour of Canary Wharf, the developers decided in 1986 to increase the gross area of development from 650,000 to 1,500,000 sq.ft.[21]

New developments were now, very largely, office

50. Thames Quay, Marsh Wall, a medium-rise commercial development of the later 1980s: north front facing the South West India Docks (see page 84).

blocks, usually built on a speculative basis, and often initially comprising medium-rise buildings. An example of this is the first phase of South Quay Plaza, begun in 1985 and completed in 1987, which for a time became the *Daily Telegraph*'s offices, designated Peterborough Court. Thames Quay, nearby, is another medium-rise development which was built in 1987–9, although plans were originally drawn up in 1985 (*50*).

This medium-rise phase was quickly followed by a high-rise one, reflecting greater confidence and increased funding from investors keen to be involved in Docklands, and influenced by the tall towers envisaged for Canary Wharf. Thus, for instance, the plans at Heron Quays were again revised in 1988, this time envisaging towers of 25 and 30 storeys, while subsequent plans, announced in 1990, proposed two sail-like towers of 36 and 46 storeys. Harbour Exchange, completed in 1990, is an example of an extensive high-rise office development, providing 1.25 million sq.ft of accommodation on a ten-acre site (*48*). In some cases the effects of these three phases of development can be seen within a single scheme. At Waterside, for instance, where work began in 1984, the first block is a two- and four-storey building of 40 small-business apartments which was completed in 1987. Then came the medium-rise Beaufort Court, Quay House and Ensign House, completed in 1987 and 1988. The final block, South Quay Waterside, is a high-rise, 24-storey office building, completed in 1992.

As developments became more and more office-orientated, not only did the scale of the buildings change, but also the smooth marble-clad and tinted-glass curtain walling, already employed by office blocks in the City and in the great international business centres throughout the world, was adopted. Richard North, commenting on this new type of Docklands building in June 1988, wrote:

They are Meccanoed together in steel frames, providing huge floor areas free of pillars. Then, to add the excitement their

51. A Contrast in Scale: No. 25 Cabot Square on Canary Wharf looms over the earlier offices of Littlejohn Frazer, completed in 1987 (see pages 63, 79).

architects aspire to, semi-circular or triangular steel work is planted on top. Often its shape-work is no more than drapery. Sometimes, there are atria: multi storey glassed spaces which might, if you were very lucky, remind you of the glass work at Kew Gardens, and the genuine fun of Decimus Burton and Joseph Paxton.

Many of the new offices have token additions of stone facing. In the case of the *Telegraph* building and its bigger brother, the thing is made to look as though its ground floor was solid stone blocks. In reality, the "blocks" are wafer thin and make arches like a stage set's.[22]

Large-scale office developments attracted a number of City businesses and institutions to the Isle of Dogs. Among firms which had their headquarters on the Island by 1990 were the Regency Life Group and two City accountants, Littlejohn Frazer and Price Waterhouse. By then, international bankers included Merrill Lynch Europe at Greenwich View, and the Italian International Bank at Heron Quays. At Coriander Avenue, just to the south of East India Dock Road, the London Telehouse had computer suites intended as data centres for international finance houses. The institutions represented included: the Association of International Bond Dealers in Limeharbour; FIMBRA – the financial regulatory body set up by the Government – at Hertsmere House; and the Stock Exchange, which had a computer centre at Greenwich View. In 1992 the Western University of Phoenix, Arizona, opened its London Business School at Glengall Bridge.[23]

Although the transfer of a major Government department to Docklands now seems unlikely (see Canary Wharf, page 60), in August 1991 the 530 staff of the Government Export Credit Guarantee department moved into Harbour Exchange,[24] and in 1992 the Department of Transport took 8,000 sq.ft at South Quay Plaza 2 for its London Docklands division. The central services of Tower Hamlets Borough Council moved to Mulberry Place on the East India Dock site in the summer of 1993.[25] After the Jubilee extension was finally approved, 2,000 London Underground staff moved into No. 30 The South Colonnade at Canary Wharf.[26]

Docklands was particularly successful in attracting newspaper and magazine publishers away from their old premises in the City or elsewhere in inner London. Quite fortuitously, the development of Docklands coincided with the moment when new technology was making possible the physical separation of editing and printing processes. This led to a mass exodus of national newspapers from their traditional locations in Fleet Street, and, as with other types of firm, the financial concessions offered by the Enterprise Zone proved a strong inducement to move to Docklands.[27] There are four such newspaper groups – *Telegraph, Express, Guardian,* and *Financial Times* – which now have printing works within the Enterprise Zone, the first two sharing premises at West Ferry Printers, and soon to be joined by the *Financial Times* (see page 86). The *Telegraph* also moved its other staff to Peterborough Court, and subsequently to Canary

52. *The Guardian* Printing Works on the Enterprise Business Park, looking north-east (see page 69).

Wharf, and in 1994 Mirror Group Newspapers moved 1,000 staff from Holborn to Canary Wharf, where they were joined in the same year by the *Independent* and *Independent on Sunday*. Other publishers to take offices in the Enterprise Zone are the Northern and Shell Group, now at City Harbour (having moved from its own building at Millharbour), Thomas Telford (the publishing offshoot of the Institution of Civil Engineers) at Heron Quays, and the Builder Group at Great Eastern Enterprise. In addition, Reuters, the international press and financial data agency, has built a data-centre on part of the Blackwall Yard site, while FT Analysis, a *Financial Times* subsidiary, providing a financial information service, moved into Telehouse Europe in 1991.[28]

Private Financing and Investment

Much of the private investment in Docklands has come from overseas, because, it has been argued, foreign investors were unaware of the problems that deterred more local investors and the prejudices against the 'East End'.[29] On the Isle of Dogs, Canary Wharf was developed by the Canadian firm Olympia & York; Japanese firms were involved at Ferguson's Wharf, Harbour Exchange, the London Telehouse, and South Quay Plaza 3; Swedish firms at the East India Dock site and the Price Waterhouse Building; a Dutch bank at City Harbour; and a Kuwaiti consortium at Meridian Gate. In October 1990 it was stated that 70 per cent of investment in Docklands had originated from overseas sources.[30]

A number of commercial developments within the Enterprise Zone have been purchased by trusts set up as tax shelters. In this way an investor who had put £10,000 into such a trust and who was paying tax at 60 per cent would immediately recoup £5,700 in tax relief. The

53. The Price Waterhouse Building, No. 161 Marsh Wall, originally intended as a Scandinavian Trade Centre. View looking south-east (see page 81).

balance could be borrowed through the trusts, and the interest payments on this also attracted tax relief. At the same time, the proportion due to the investor of rents from the property purchased by the trust might provide the repayments on any such loan. Thus, a series of Property Enterprise Trusts (PETs) was set up by Rutland Trust, which purchased buildings at Harbour Exchange, as well as the Price Waterhouse Building and part of Nos 30–40 Marsh Wall. In the same way, Laser (London and South-East Enterprise Zone Real Property) Trusts were launched by Colegrave Johnson Fry (subsequently Johnson Fry), which purchased Harbour Island (at Harbour Exchange), the Isis and Wallbrook Buildings at Thames Quay, another part of Nos 30–40 Marsh Wall, and five buildings on the western phase of Glengall Bridge.[31]

The commercial development of Docklands also coincided with the introduction to the British property market, in the mid-1980s, of 'off-balance-sheet financing'. In simple terms, a company first decided to engage a partner to share the risk of development. They then set up an associate company, off their own balance sheets, whose sole asset was the development. This associated company raised finance against the security of the development, so that there was no liability on the developers, except, for instance, when cost or construction time overran. The developers entered into construction contracts at a fixed price. Finally, the developers sought to lease the building to a company before it was completed, or arranged to sell it once it had been completed. In this way a profit of about 20 per cent of the value might be obtained. Should the project fail it was the financiers, not the developers, who were left with a half-finished, unlet, or unsold building.[32] At South Quay Plaza 3 the joint developers, Marples International and National Leasing & Finance, set up special companies to carry out this development – Notchmixi and Gablewide – and these companies were financed by an international syndicate of banks.[33]

Reaction and Recession

As the pace of development on the Isle of Dogs quickened and investors became increasingly eager to back schemes in the area, so land prices rose rapidly: in 1981 land values averaged £50,000 an acre, by March 1988 these had increased tenfold, with waterside sites fetching over £1 million per acre, and some particularly prime sites reaching as much as £10 million an acre.[34] Yet commercial rents remained much lower than comparable rents in the City. In 1988, when top rents for offices on the Isle of Dogs were £20 per sq.ft, those in the City were £60 per sq.ft.[35] Rents remained lower on the Isle of Dogs, even after 26 April 1992, when properties became liable to pay the local Uniform Business Rate.[36]

The original concept of Docklands was as an area of fairly small-scale developments, with cheaply constructed high-tech buildings, which, as the need arose, were capable of a variety of uses. They were designed to be relatively temporary in nature, so that they could either be re-sited (as happened to the Ladkarn Building, see page 78) or demolished to make way for a different type of development (54). Canary Wharf and its many imitators brought an end to this flexible approach and established the Isle of Dogs as an area predominantly of office blocks. The dangers of this were already becoming apparent early in 1988, when it was predicted that the office market in the Isle of Dogs would soon become flooded. According to the *Daily Telegraph*:

So far only around one million square feet of offices have been completed, and of that less than 800,000 is occupied. Little space will be completed this year. The build-up begins in 1989 when over two million square feet will be completed, with massive floor area coming on to the market in 1990–1992.[37]

54. Disposable Buildings: the Ladkarn Building, West India Docks, constructed in 1985, was dismantled two years later and re-erected at Beckton (see page 78).

Also, the challenge presented by Canary Wharf immediately persuaded the City to relax its planning controls in 1985, allowing the creation of developments over roads and railways and on sites previously regarded as inviolable, so that another 20 million sq.ft of office development was added within the Square Mile.[38] As a result, by the end of 1993, half the City's stock of office accommodation had been built since 1986.[39] Similarly, the City of Westminster encouraged prestige developments, such as the world's largest financial dealing room above Victoria Station.[40] Furthermore, during 1987 and 1988 the Government introduced a general relaxation of planning regulations, allowing industrial or warehousing premises to be changed to offices without requiring planning permission, and thus taking away one of the distinctive advantages of an Enterprise Zone.[41] So, by the late 1980s, Docklands was in direct competition with the City and other inner London areas to fill new office blocks. During 1989 some rents began to drop to about £16 per sq.ft, as developers tried to attract tenants.[42] Among the financial incentives then on offer in Docklands were free fitting out of accommodation, six-month rent-free periods, and other rental agreements advantageous to tenants.[43] By October of that year it was claimed that 'it is probably true that with such a vast amount of space coming on to the market in Docklands nowhere else in Greater London can a prospective occupier negotiate such a comprehensive package of inducements'.[44]

By April 1990 the *Daily Telegraph* was noting that: 'The property market in London's Docklands has marked time over the last six months with only a handful of lettings to companies not already represented in the enterprise zone'.[45] By November 1990 there was 1.4 million sq.ft of vacant commercial property available in the Isle of Dogs.[46] In the same year receivers were called in at South Quay Plaza 3, where the development companies found it difficult to let this phase of the scheme, and failed to keep up with their interest payments.[47] Similarly, in March 1990 the shares of the developer of South Quay Waterside were suspended, and part of the development had to be quickly sold off and the financial arrangements for the rest restructured to allow completion of the scheme.[48] Yet in both instances the first phases had been very successful. At Skylines, where again the original part was sold very quickly, the last stage has proved much more difficult to dispose of. By February 1991 vacancy rates in the Enterprise Zone were running at about 50 per cent, and only Canary Wharf was regarded as part of the Central London commercial property market.[49]

In the same month, office space at South Quay Plaza 3 was being offered at just £10 per sq.ft (compared with about £30 in West London and £40 in the City), yet even at this price it failed to attract tenants.[50] An earlier and more modest building – Parker House, at nearby Waterside – was available in April 1991 for £5 per sq.ft.[51] At the same time, the Isis building at Thames Quay was offered with a two-year rent-free period and no obligation for a tenant to remain in the building after that date. In the summer of 1992, according to the *Estates Times*, accommodation was let at South Quay Plaza 2 at a rent equating to 'substantially less' than £5 per sq.ft.[52]

By the spring of 1991 those seeking smaller accommodation could find sufficient cheap premises in the City and only larger users were still considering Docklands.[53] Fears began to be expressed that the Isle of Dogs had become too dominated by offices, such specialization leaving it vulnerable to economic decline, and the LDDC revised its development plans in order to get a greater mix of uses in the future.[54] The glut in office accommodation appeared to be much greater than that in residential property and existed throughout the whole of the London region. In May 1992 about 20 million sq.ft of office space was available in the City, and 14 million sq.ft was on the market in London's West End.[55] Indeed, conditions were such that in 1992–3 it was being predicted by property experts that the chances of letting some office accommodation in London during the next ten years or more were extremely slim.[56]

Most worrying for the long-term future is the nature of this new office accommodation. Much of it was specifically intended for the financial services industry in the wake of the 1986 'Big Bang' (see page 48). The offices are, therefore, designed to meet the needs of the new technology, with floor-to-floor heights one-and-a-half times greater than a normal office block. This allows the accommodation of air-conditioning with twice the usual power, an electricity supply with three times the regular capacity to run the computers, higher floor loadings, and large unobstructed floors.[57] Yet the pace of technological advance has been so rapid that by 1991 it was argued that such office blocks had become largely obsolete and, especially with the decline in the financial services industry, no longer met the current requirements of the commercial property market.[58]

In a reversal of what had happened in Docklands a few years before, developers began to consider converting commercial space to residential accommodation, as that market seemed likely to recover more quickly. At South Quay Waterside the developers explored the possibility of converting the small-business suites into student accommodation, with about 1,000 bedrooms, but by May 1995 this scheme had not been implemented.[59]

From 26 April 1992, the Isle of Dogs lost its Enterprise Zone status. The most serious blow, for developers still struggling to let commercial property, was that they then had to pay 50 per cent of the Uniform Business Rate on any empty buildings, amounting to about £3.50 per sq.ft at that time.[60]

Yet, despite this, by 1995 there is evidence that the commercial, like the housing, property market is gradually beginning to recover. With so much existing vacant property, no new commercial developments are yet under way, but the low rents offered in Docklands (for example, in May 1995 the Innovation Centre, Marsh Wall, was advertising space at £3 per square foot per annum) are attracting firms to relocate there rather than in the City.[61]

Gazetteer of Commercial, Industrial, and other Non-housing Developments

The numbers in the margins identify the location of the developments as shown on the plan on page 21.

1 *Advance House, No. 33 Millharbour*

This is a high-tech 'shiny shed', with silver corrugated cladding, red panels and black glass (*back cover*). It was developed by Advanced Textile Products for its own use, designed by Nicholas Lacey, Jobst & Hyett, and was completed in 1987, with Henry Davis & Company as the project managers and Jarvis as the builders. There are 30,000 sq.ft of office space on three floors, and ware-housing is provided.[62]

4 *ASDA Superstore*

The superstore, off East Ferry Road, was the first major modern retail development on the Isle of Dogs. In the early 1980s part of the site of the Transporter Yard to the north of the Mudchute was leased from the PLA by the Leeds-based Associated Dairies, who were seeking to build a ring of supermarkets around outer London. The Isle of Dogs store was designed by the Whittam Cox Ellis Clayton Partnership,[63] and was built by Wates Construction in 1981–3.[64] The cost of development was reported to be £6 million, the total area is 97,000 sq.ft, and the store opened with more than 300 employees.[65] There is an internal row of nine smaller, independent shops (plus one external shop), a cafeteria, a filling station and 600 parking spaces.[66] The store is a low, single-storey, flat-roofed building, with a square tower, topped by a pyramidal slated roof, set towards the north-west corner. The building is faced in dark-red mottled brick, with black ribbed fascias and light-green metalwork. Inside, the metal, latticed, roof-girders are exposed.

7 *The Business Centre, Dollar Bay*

This was developed by Dysart Developments and Ladkarn Holdings, with the Beaton Thomas Partnership as architects. The first phase, constructed by Costain in 1990–2, is a 350-space public car park. Two five-storey office blocks (Sovereign and Sterling Houses, providing 5,610 sq.m and 5,405 sq.m respectively) are planned, but work had not begun on site by May 1995.[67]

9 *Canary Wharf*

This is the largest and most important development in modern Docklands (*55, 56, 61*). Indeed, to many contemporary observers, the ultimate fortunes of the whole area depend upon its success or failure.

Development of the site began modestly enough, with the conversion in 1982–3 of one of the existing warehouses (No. 30 Shed) into Limehouse Studios (see page

78). Then, in 1984 the LDDC gave permission for more ambitious plans for the central warehouse (No. 31 Shed) at Canary Wharf. Under this scheme, designed by Architects Workshop (George Finch and Bob Giles), the existing building would have been converted into 83 dwellings, and 65 shells for shops, offices and cafés, all above a station of the proposed Docklands Light Railway. The estimated cost was £10 million. Interestingly, even at this stage a grand tree-lined boulevard and a formal garden were proposed.[68]

However, these proposals were swept away by plans on a much grander scale, which were approved by the LDDC in October 1985. The new plans envisaged a £1.5 billion development on the site, for 10 million sq.ft of office, hotel and retail space.[69] The consortium backing this scheme was led by G. Ware Travelstead, an American developer and principal of First Boston Real Estate. His attention had been drawn to Canary Wharf by Michael Van Clemm of the American bankers, Crédit Suisse First Boston, on whose behalf Travelstead had been negotiating unsuccessfully for four years trying to find a major re-development for them in the City of London. They were joined in the consortium by Morgan Stanley, another American investment bank, and both intended that the scheme should include new headquarters buildings for themselves.[70]

At this stage there were plans for three tower blocks, each 850ft high, as well as lower blocks, and it was optimistically thought that the first phase, including one of the very tall blocks, might be completed by the end of 1988.[71] The general site plan and infrastructure were designed by the American practices of Skidmore, Owings & Merrill (project architect Bruce Graham) and I. M. Pei (project architect Henry Cobb), in association with the British firm of Yorke, Rosenberg and Mardall.[72]

There was considerable opposition to the prospect of three such high tower blocks, especially as they would loom large in views from Greenwich Park, although the simplified planning procedures within the Enterprise Zone prevented such opinions being presented formally, and equally precluded the Secretary of State for the Environment from holding a public inquiry into the matter.[73] In 1986 a group of local authorities, led by the GLC and the Borough of Greenwich, tried to get a judicial review of the scheme, but failed.[74] Tower Hamlets Borough Council, on the other hand, was generally in favour of the plans and the prospect of local jobs that they offered.[75] Some commentators, most notably Colin Amery in the *Financial Times*, welcomed the tall towers, and the Royal Fine Art Commission also accepted them, although with reservations about their positioning.[76]

Initial work on the infrastructure for the site was completed early in 1987, but the master building agreement between the LDDC and the Canary Wharf consortium had still not been signed by April of that year. A month later the Conservative Government was returned for a third term, and resolved to break the deadlock by fixing a tight deadline for the signing of the agreement. This forced Travelstead to accept that he was unable to

55. Canary Wharf: aerial view of the development in September 1991. The first phase, including the Canary Wharf Tower, has been completed, but the second phase beside Westferry Circus is still under construction.

assemble the necessary funding for such an enormous scheme,[77] and in July 1987 Morgan Stanley and Crédit Suisse First Boston withdrew from the consortium.[78]

From the outset there had been scepticism that such an ambitious scheme could ever be realized,[79] and it seemed these doubts were to be quickly confirmed. However, the Chairman of the LDDC, Christopher Benson, approached the Canadian-based Olympia & York, with whom his company, MEPC, had had dealings in the early 1980s.[80] Olympia & York had become one of the largest developers and owners of office properties in North America. Its prosperity was largely based on an ability to spot the possibilities of apparently unpromising sites, offered at low prices. The money saved on land-purchase was then spent on erecting good-quality buildings and creating pleasant environments, which attracted top firms as tenants. In this way the firm had developed Flemington Park in Toronto and the World Financial Center in New York, laying the basis for its enormous wealth. Seeking another site for major redevelopment, Olympia & York's criteria were apparently met by Canary Wharf.

They took over the scheme almost immediately and completed the master agreement on time.[81]

As a private company, owned by the brothers Paul, Arthur and Ralph Reichmann (with Paul as the dominant figure), Olympia & York[a] were particularly suited to execute such a scheme, for, as the magazine *Business* remarked: 'no public company answering to shareholders and bankers would have dared to be so ambitious'.[83] Or put the other way: 'Paul Reichmann's exalted reputation was the cornerstone of Canary Wharf. Had the project been championed by any other developer in the world, it almost certainly would have expired on the drawing board.'[84] Moreover, by appearing as the last-minute saviour of a floundering project, it put itself in a very strong position for negotiations with the LDDC and the Government. In particular, the price for the site was very advantageous to Olympia & York. According to the LDDC, 'The price paid for the 20 acres of LDDC-owned land on Canary Wharf equates to £1 million per acre of which £8 million is payable in cash and £12 million is represented by the developers' commitments to

---

[a] The first component alludes to Paul Reichmann's interest in Greek mythology and the second to an area of Toronto.[82]

56. Canary Wharf and Heron Quays looking north-east from Cascades.

various on-site works of public benefit'.[85] In a hostile study of the scheme, the Docklands Consultative Committee argued that £1 million per acre was, by April 1987, lower than average for the Isle of Dogs. Furthermore, it claimed that the 'on-site works of public benefit', consisting of public spaces, internal roads and riverside walkways, were necessary components of the development and were eligible for tax breaks. If this was the case, then 'O & Y paid £400,000 per acre for LDDC-owned land'. In addition, the Consultative Committee pointed out that the Canary Wharf Master Plan created an extra 26 acres by building over the water in the docks. Since these also belonged to the LDDC and were not mentioned in the July 1987 press release, the Consultative Committee concluded that 'O & Y paid £8 million for 46 acres, an average of less than £174,000 an acre'.[86]

Olympia & York generally made only minor changes to the original scheme, but the tower blocks were repositioned and the two easternmost ones were reduced in height.[87] One other significant alteration was the abandonment of the raised pedestrian deck that covered most of the site in the original plan for Travelstead.[88] Skidmore, Owings & Merrill also drew up design guidelines which were incorporated into the purchase contract of the site from the LDDC. These laid down design constraints for each individual building, giving maximum dimensions, heights of setbacks, cornice lines, and the locations of arcades.[89]

The detailed master-plan and guidelines allowed a number of architects to be employed on the different sites, while guaranteeing that the overall concept would be adhered to. Also, developers received automatic planning permission provided they conformed to the guidelines.[90] There was less concern about stipulating building materials for façades, except that bases were to be primarily of natural stone and, most importantly, the use of mirror-reflective glass was banned.[91] In late 1988 and early 1989 two major master-plan meetings were held, involving all the architects concerned, when final decisions were made over such things as the colours of stone to be used, the types of glass, and the heights and setbacks of the different blocks.[92]

The total area of the Canary Wharf site is 71 acres[93] but, under Olympia & York, plans grew to encompass adjacent sites (*57*). To the north, seven acres at Port East was intended to have shops, restaurants, leisure and entertainment facilities, a hotel, offices and car parking, while, to the south, 15 acres at Heron Quays was to be

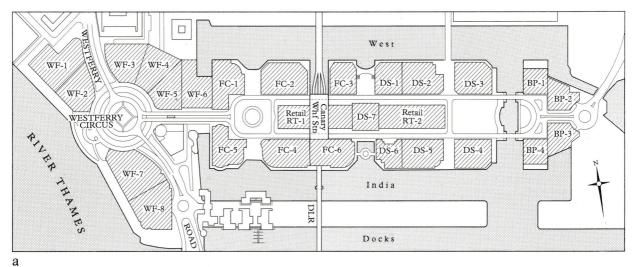

57. Canary Wharf

(a) Olympia & York's development plan of 1988. The proposed buildings are hatched and were intended for office use except where indicated.

(b) Plan showing the state of development in March 1993 (completed buildings are hatched) and areas of possible future development, including Port East to the north and Heron Quays to the south.

devoted mainly to residential use. The developers proclaimed that 'interconnected by pedestrian bridges, road and rail links, Port East and Heron Quays will create an integrated commercial and residential district with Canary Wharf'.[94] These plans were shelved when those for the later phases of Canary Wharf were suspended.

Lehrer McGovern Bovis, a company formed in 1986 by a merger of the British contractors Bovis and Lehrer McGovern, a similar New York firm, were appointed as general construction managers for Canary Wharf.[95] An area where Olympia & York had previously proved astute in saving money was in the use of a special vertical lift system which drastically cut the number of man-hours involved in the erection of tall buildings. This system, utilized at Canary Wharf, provided a work-station that could rise with the building and was equipped with a canteen, lavatories and a store for building materials.[96] Construction under Olympia & York began in November 1987.[97] The first phase of development, consisting of the western end of the site, and straddling the Docklands Light Railway, was begun in May 1988, when the first pile for the first building was sunk by the Prime Minister,

Margaret Thatcher. At the time Paul Reichmann admitted that his firm 'would not be making a commitment of this magnitude' without 'the inspiration and wholehearted support' of the Government.[98] Apart from No. 1 Cabot Square and Cabot Place, all the buildings in phase one are largely built over water in the dock, using steel piles (with base-grouted bored piles being used on land).[99]

At the height of construction activity in late 1989 and early 1990 there were nearly 4,500 people working on site.[100] Because the site was very narrow (only 116m wide) and almost surrounded by water, it was too cramped to store any materials. A six-hectare storage yard was therefore set up at Tilbury Docks and 85 per cent of the building materials for the first phase were shipped by barge from there to the dock site. Some 200,000 cu.m of material excavated on site for foundations and facilities were also taken away by barge. When building work was at its most intense, 80 barges were employed in transporting materials to or from the site, and there were more than 500 barge movements a month. Further barges were anchored alongside the quay to provide site offices, medical facilities, and a canteen, while there was also a floating concrete plant. A series of temporary roads, designed by Ove Arup, was built over the water in the dock, with piles driven into the river-bed to support a steel deck. Despite all this, Olympia & York estimated before work began that 64,000 truck loads of material, 40,000 of them of concrete, would have to be brought by road, and construction traffic for Canary Wharf temporarily aggravated the difficulties of vehicles trying to get on and off the Isle of Dogs.[101]

The contract to build the infrastructure for phase one, representing 16 separate projects (including roads and landscaping), was awarded to Bovis Construction. It was worth more than £200 million.[102] The ambitious landscaping is a notable feature of the scheme, all the more remarkable in that it sits on top of five levels of car parking and services. The master-plan provides for more than 25 acres of squares, parks, boulevards and waterside promenades throughout the entire site. When the first phase was opened to the public in the summer of 1991, the buildings stood in a mature landscape. The Philadelphia-based landscape architect, Laurie Olin of Hanna-Olin, was responsible for working out the horticultural details, and Sir Roy Strong, former director of the Victoria and Albert Museum, acted as design consultant. More than 400 mature trees (900 are intended for the whole site) of 20 species, over 2,300 shrubs in more than 90 varieties, and 83,500 spring and autumn flowering bulbs were planted. The placing of the trees and shrubs was, in part, intended to create a wind-break and give protection to a potentially bleak and exposed site. Decorative features include the gates and railings at Westferry Circus by Giuseppe Lund, symbolizing the seasons (58), further railings on Wren Landing by Bruce McLean, and a computer-controlled fountain in Cabot Square by Bruce Chaix, capable of performing 42 different water 'dances' (62). The ventilator shafts from the underground car

parks are encased in sculpted cast-glass panels by Jeff Bell. Most of the street furniture, such as telephone kiosks, bus shelters, bicycle-stands, lamp-posts and rubbish bins, was specially designed by Skidmore, Owings & Merrill, but the benches are by Wales & Wales.[103]

The first phase was completed in 1991, and the first tenants moved into the main tower that August.[104] As far as retail provision was concerned, there was a deliberate attempt to attract 'speciality shops' of sufficient quality to appeal to the employees of big corporations.[105] The first retail outlet opened in October 1991, by December of that year 14 shops and restaurants, plus a public house, were trading, and by August 1992 the number had risen to 20, with a further two let (59, 60).[106] Although in March 1994 most of the shopping activity was concentrated in Cabot Place West, by the end of that year the majority of the retail units on the ground and first floors at Cabot Place East were also open for trading, and in February 1995 a Tesco Metro store was opened on the first floor at Cabot Place West. Elsewhere on the development, even in May 1995, despite the large number of retail units available, there was only one shop open, together with two public houses and five restaurants.

In 1990 there were signs, hardly noticed at the time, that even Olympia & York was beginning to be affected by an almost world-wide property slump and the rise in interest rates. During that year the company found itself encumbered with a loan of $260 million from the

58. Westferry Circus: gate and railings designed by Giuseppe Lund.

59. Canary Wharf: shopping colonnade on the ground floor of Nos. 5 and 10 Cabot Square, looking east.

bankrupt Campeau Corporation, it was only able to pay $200 million of a $550-million loan to Japan's Sanwa Bank, and it tried to sell 20 per cent of its American property.[107] In 1990 the development of Canary Wharf produced an operating loss of £160 million.[108] In May 1991 the three later phases of the development there were halted until further notice, and some staff were laid off.[109] By then Olympia & York, with its interests in New York, London and Toronto, was seen to be dangerously exposed in a falling property market,[110] and in August 1991 $100 million of Olympia & York debentures were downgraded because of the real-estate slump.[111] Unfortunately for the company, its other investments were in industries such as oil and paper, which were equally badly hit by the recession.[112]

Not the least of Olympia & York's problems was the failure to attract sufficient tenants for the first phase of Canary Wharf. Most of those persuaded to take accommodation in the development were offered various inducements. In part this may be seen as a sign of increasing desperation on the part of the company, but Olympia & York had already used a similar technique with great success at its World Finance Center development in Manhattan. The philosophy was that a few prestigious clients attracted others, encouraged further investment, quickly established the development as a good address, and allowed later lettings to be at much higher prices.[113]

The *Daily Telegraph* group was persuaded to move into Canary Wharf Tower after Olympia & York paid £40 million for its headquarters at Peterborough Court, South Quay Plaza, giving the group a £15 million profit at a time when property prices were at rock bottom.[114] In other cases Olympia & York is said to have agreed to pay for the fitting out of offices, rent-free periods of up to four years, and the taking over of leases on firms' existing premises.[115] According to the *Evening Standard*, 'that has left them with an estimated 250,000 square feet of space . . . most of which is empty . . . Servicing costs on these exchange deals are estimated to be adding another £10 million a month to Olympia & York's outgoings on Canary Wharf'.[116] By March 1992, despite fierce marketing, Canary Wharf was only 60 per cent let.[117] Significantly, Olympia & York had failed to persuade any major British firm to move to the development, other than the *Daily Telegraph*.[118]

The company's problems quickly became acute after a number of its debt issues were downgraded in Toronto in February 1992.[119] This caused nervousness in the financial market, making it difficult for Olympia & York to refinance short-term debts, and its bankers began to question the company's financial soundness.[120] With debts to the banks estimated to be £11.5 billion, Olympia & York had urgent talks with a number of British and American financial institutions. At this stage the Bank of England intervened to persuade a group of clearing banks, led by Barclays and Lloyds, to provide Canary Wharf with an emergency loan of £52 million.[121] Discussions with the banks were carried on through April and into early May.[122] In the meantime, Olympia & York's general financial problems continued, on top of which the firm was losing £48 million a month at Canary Wharf,[123] and, from late April, when the Enterprise Zone status of the Isle of Dogs ended, having to pay half the Uniform Business Rate on its empty buildings.

By early May 1992 Olympia & York had run out of money to continue Canary Wharf, and work was only kept going on a week-to-week basis by the syndicate of 11 banks backing the scheme.[124] Later in the month the company and 32 of its subsidiaries filed for bankruptcy protection in Canada and the USA.[125] At the time, it was trying to obtain money to finish off the second phase of Canary Wharf, but what particularly disturbed the scheme's bankers was that much of the money required was simply to pay interest on existing loans,[126] and in late May Canary Wharf was handed over to an accountancy firm, Ernst & Young, who were appointed as administrators by the banks.[127]

In general terms and with the advantage of hindsight, it is possible to suggest some of the reasons why Canary Wharf contributed to Olympia & York's downfall. In the first place, the Reichmanns, guided by their previous successes, failed to see that there were important differences between Canary Wharf and the sites which they had developed with some notable success in North America. In American cities and towns it has been relatively easy to establish suburban developments, whereas in Europe there has been much more resistance from firms and their

60. Canary Wharf: shopping mall in Cabot Place West.

workers to decentralization. This is largely due to the richness of commercial, social and cultural life which has evolved over the centuries in the centres of Europe's very much older main towns and cities.[128] Also, new suburban developments in North America have depended upon quick and easy transport communications. From the outset, under Travelstead, it had been realized that road and rail access to Canary Wharf had to be drastically improved.[129] Olympia & York, coming from a different culture, failed to appreciate how long it would take to get the necessary financial backing and Government approval for the new transport schemes.

Perhaps the biggest mistake, and one which had serious repercussions for the whole Enterprise Zone, was the way in which the Canary Wharf scheme was promoted as a direct challenge to the City of London. From the outset, Travelstead was proclaiming the planned development as an alternative financial centre far superior to the Square Mile.[130] Again, coming from another culture, the Reichmanns failed to realize just how fiercely, over the years, the City has defended its position as a national and international financial centre. It reacted swiftly in the face of this blatant challenge (see page 52).

Moreover, the type of accommodation provided was already becoming dated by the time the first part of the development had been completed (see page 52). To *The Times* it seemed that 'far too much had been spent on constructing the most opulent and sophisticated office complex in Europe on a site that could never justify such investment'.[131]

The administrators of Canary Wharf were given £10 million – enough to keep work on the project going for about two weeks.[132] They were required to seek a buyer for the development, and there was initial optimism. Indeed, Sheik Maktoum al Maktoum of Dubai, one of the world's richest men, had reportedly offered to buy the development before Olympia & York relinquished control, but was said to have withdrawn when the Government refused to extend the Enterprise Zone status of the Isle of Dogs by an extra five years.[133] After the site went into administration a number of possible buyers were mentioned in the press, including the Hong Kong billionaire Li Ka-Shing,[134] the Dudley-based property developers Roy and Don Richardson,[135] the P & O Group,[136] British Land[137] and, most persistently, Lord Hanson.[138] Paul Reichmann even assembled a consortium of investors – including CBS, Lewis Ranier, the Wall Street investor, and Primerica, the American insurance group – to bid for the development.[139] In late August 1992 ten parties were said to be considering making offers for Canary Wharf.[140]

In fact, the chances of finding a buyer for such a large development, encumbered with debt, at a time when the property market was showing no signs of recovery, were always remote – especially if Olympia & York, with all its resources, experience and flair had failed. What further bedevilled the matter was the impossibility of solving the triangular conundrum which had developed over Canary Wharf. Following preliminary pronouncements, it was confirmed in June 1992 that 2,000 staff from the Department of the Environment's offices in Marsham Street, Westminster, were to be relocated in Docklands (several possible venues were suggested but Canary Wharf was regarded as the most likely).[141] There was still a problem, however, which was that the Government would not guarantee the move of one of its major departments to Canary Wharf without the Jubilee Line extension being built, yet it was unwilling to sanction the construction of the line without the contribution from the private sector promised by Olympia & York (see page 18), but any potential purchaser of Canary Wharf was likely to want a firm commitment that the Government would move staff there and would give the go-ahead for the Jubilee Line. In the negotiations which ensued a battle of nerves developed between the administrators and the Government: the administrators hoped the Government would feel politically obliged to sanction the Jubilee Line extension and the staff move, while the Government remained adamant that it would commit itself to neither until the private sector guaranteed the agreed contribution to the extension.

In October 1992 the Canary Wharf administrators announced that they had found a buyer prepared to pay the £98 million for the block intended to house the civil servants, provided the Government would guarantee the move. This sum would then have provided the first contribution by Canary Wharf's bankers to the Jubilee Line extension. However, this failed to meet the Government's approval, and later in the month it was announced that the Department of the Environment's staff would, in fact, remain at Marsham Street for the time being.[142] Probably the Government was relieved to drop the matter, since there had been considerable opposition to relocation, not least from the Civil Service unions, who organized a one-day strike,[143] and from the City of Westminster, which protested about the damage such a move would do to the prosperity of its own area.[144] Finally, in November, the Canary Wharf bankers were persuaded to put up money for the Jubilee Line extension unconditionally and, on this basis, the Government agreed that construction would proceed (see page 18).[145]

In the latter part of 1992 Canary Wharf continued to absorb monthly administrative fees of £400,000,[146] although the rents from existing tenants were sufficient to allow the administrators to run all of the services and maintain security.[147] In April 1993 the European Investment Bank agreed to give a loan of £98 million for the Jubilee Line extension, in return for a stake in Canary Wharf. This led, in October, to the approval of a rescue scheme worth £1.1 billion, which allowed Canary Wharf to be taken out of administration. The development's assets were transferred to a successor company, Sylvester Investments,[b] formed by the, now 12, banks, which in turn set up a new management company responsible for

[b] Sylvester is the cartoon cat who is always trying to catch the canary, Tweety Pie.

61. Canary Wharf seen from Rotherhithe. On the right is Cascades and part of The Anchorage.

the day-to-day running of the project, headed by Sir Peter Levene, then Chairman of the Docklands Light Railway. Since then further lettings have been made (although the two most recent have been to banks already involved with the development, Barclays and Morgan Stanley), and 72 per cent of Canary Wharf (3.3 million sq.ft) had been let by May 1995.[148] It is hoped to complete the rest of the development, albeit at a slower pace than previously planned.[149] Yet, if Canary Wharf has not proved an immediate financial success, its physical embodiment is an impressive tribute to North American optimism and methods of construction.

The following buildings and structures have been erected so far (their original designations are given in brackets where appropriate):

Westferry Circus, at the western end of the site, is a circular, two-tier structure, designed by Skidmore, Owings & Merrill (*55, 58*). At ground level is a covered traffic-roundabout, with approach and departure roads rising up to the main site, and above is a large landscaped open space. Construction was carried out in 1987–91 by Canary Wharf Contractors (a consortium of Taylor Woodrow, Tarmac, Costain, Mowlem and Sir Robert McAlpine), at a cost of £40 million.[150]

Trafalgar Way leads southwards off the Preston's Road roundabout, forms the eastern access to Canary Wharf, and was built by the LDDC. The northern half was completed in 1988 and the southern section (at a cost of £7.69 million) in 1990.[151]

No. 1 Cabot Square (FC1) was designed by Pei Cobb Freed & Partners for Crédit Suisse First Boston as their headquarters, and the management contractors were Ellis Don and Robert McAlpine. The block is stepped-back in several stages, but otherwise the façades are unremitting combinations of rectangular windows and precast panels of white Jura Limestone, relieved only by bands of grey America jet mist granite from Georgia. The building, which is the tallest on the site after Canary Wharf Tower, rises to 18 storeys (plus 2 storeys of plant at the top), and has a two-storey arcade at the base, to Cabot Square. In the event, Crédit Suisse First Boston took only about 170,000 sq.ft, approximately one-third of the total of 557,000 sq.ft of accommodation, and by the autumn of 1991 ownership had passed to Glenstreet Property Development.[152]

No. 10 Cabot Square (FC2) (also incorporating No. 5 Cabot Square) was designed by Skidmore, Owings & Merrill, and erected by Bovis Construction, at a reported cost of about £105 million (*62*). This is a 10- and 12-storey block in a monumental Transatlantic neo-Classical style, giving 60,700 sq.m of office space. It has a stainless-steel pitched roof, and is clad with yellow bricks set in precast-concrete panels, and Portland stone precast-concrete details, manufactured in Belgium. A ground-floor

62. Canary Wharf: Nos. 5 and 10 Cabot Square looking north-east across the square and the computer-controlled fountain designed by Bruce Chaix.

arcade runs along The North Colonnade and round towards Wren Landing, with teak-and-glass-fronted shops and ornate pendant lamps (*59*). Canary Wharf's second public house, the Cat and Canary, at the north-west corner of this block, was opened by Fuller's the brewers in 1992, at a cost of £700,000, and it has since been joined by a restaurant. But none of the shop units had opened by May 1995. Inside the building is an impressive three-tier, nine-storey atrium, faced and floored in marble, with bronze grilles to the balcony.[153]

No. 25 The North Colonnade (FC3) had been envisaged by Skidmore, Owings & Merrill, in their master-plan, as a mirror image of No. 10 Cabot Square, with the DLR passing between the matching pair of buildings, as it does on the south side of the wharf. Olympia & York,

however, wished to round off the first phase of construction with a Modern-style building, to give the impression that the development had not all been built at the same time. Also, by employing a British practice, it hoped to diffuse growing criticism that all the design work at Canary Wharf was going to North American architects. The building, therefore, was designed by Troughton-McAslan Ltd, a British practice, but with Adamson Associates as executive architects. The latter, based in New York, were experts on office-block design and were responsible for the technical planning and details required. The management contractor was Mowlem and the cost of constructing the shell and core was about £45 million. The 15-storey building, providing 34,000 sq.m of accommodation, has a central concrete slipformed core, which provides lateral stability and houses lifts and services. Steelwork springs from the core to support the floors. The cladding consists of a curtain wall of glass and Canadian grey-granite panels, and the block has a flat roof. The building is the most overtly Modern in style, albeit in the tradition of Owen Williams's 'Daily Express' buildings of the 1930s. Two wings are linked by entrance spaces, lift lobbies and a reception area, and there is a north-south axis through to a 'watercourt promenade'. The block was still empty in May 1995.[154]

No. 20 Cabot Square (FC4) (also incorporates No. 10 South Colonnade) was designed by the American firm of Kohn, Pedersen, Fox, in association with EPR Partnership; the management contractor was Mowlem. It is a 12-plus-2-storey building, with 52,500 sq.m of lettable space, including two overheight floors designed to be dealing rooms. The exterior, clad in white-veined Vermont marble over a steel frame, matches No. 30 The South Colonnade on the other side of the Docklands Light Railway. There is a curved face to the dockside and a circular tower at the north-west corner overlooking Cabot Square. The block is smooth and monumental, in a style which suggests streamlined Classicism, without actually having any overt Classical features. A ground-floor arcade on the north side contains shop units, but in May 1995 only one was open for business. In addition, two restaurants flank Canary Wharf's first public house (opened in September 1991), the Henry Addington.[c] This is situated at the south-west corner of the building and was fitted out for Bass Taverns.[155]

No. 30 The South Colonnade (FC6) was designed by Kohn, Pedersen, Fox, in association with EPR Partnership, and the managing contractor was Trollope & Colls (Trafalgar House Construction Management). It is a 12-plus-2-storey building facing No. 20 Cabot Square, of which it is a similar but smaller version, with a lettable area of 28,000 sq.m.[156] No retail units in this block had been taken by May 1995.

No. 25 Cabot Square (FC5) was designed by Skidmore, Owings & Merrill for Morgan Stanley International as their headquarters building (*51*). However, in 1990 Morgan Stanley and Olympia & York came to an agreement, whereby the latter bought the property and then leased it back to Morgan Stanley. The management contractor was Wimpey Tishman, and construction cost about £95 million. The 42,000-sq.m building rises to 9 and 14-plus-2-storeys. It is faced in a mixture of natural and artificial stone and marble in brown and white, with hardwood grilles. It has the look of the turn-of-the-century stripped-Classical commercial buildings by Louis H. Sullivan in Chicago. Again, there is a ground-floor arcade with retail units, but none was open in May 1995, although two restaurants were trading by then.[157]

No. 1 Canada Square (DS7), popularly known as Canary Wharf Tower, was designed by Cesar Pelli, an Argentinian-born architect, based in New Haven, Connecticut, who had already designed the buildings at the World Finance Center in Manhattan for Olympia & York. Two other architectural practices – Adamson Associates, and Frederick Gibberd Coombes & Partners – were also involved in the design and execution of the Canary Wharf building. Construction began in the spring of 1988. Initially the management contractors were Sir Robert McAlpine & Sons in association with Ellis Don of Toronto, but in April 1990, with work well behind schedule, Lehrer McGovern took over direct management of the tower's construction, although the original contractors continued to work on the building. Even so, the building was completed in August 1991, only about a month later than planned, construction having taken under three-and-a-half years, a remarkably short period for such a tall building. The cost of erection was estimated at just over £200 million.

The 50-storey tower, at 824ft the tallest building in Britain and the second tallest in Europe, is clad in stainless steel, specially produced in Panteg, Wales (*55, 61, 63*). The architect insisted on using steel for the cladding, although Olympia & York had been keen to face the tower in stone, like the other buildings on the site. Commenting on his design, Pelli said: 'It is the simplest, most pure, most basic form I have designed. It was important to me that it should be a skyscraper, not simply a high-rise building . . . I wanted it to look un-American, to step outside the three main styles of Classical, Gothic and Art Deco.' However, when the building was completed he did reveal that he had had to take off five floors in order to comply with air-traffic-safety regulations. Olympia & York were unwilling to lose any floorspace because of this and extra accommodation had to be added to the remaining floors. As a result, Pelli felt that the proportions of the block had suffered. The building provides 1.3 million sq.ft of office space, served by 32 passenger lifts. The three-storey entrance lobby is clad in a combination of black, grey, red and green marbles from Turkey, Italy and Guatemala.

Canary Wharf Tower, although it has its critics, has generally been applauded and has quickly established itself as one of London's most instantly recognisable landmarks. Seen from a distance it dominates the skyline and looks every inch of its height, and viewed from Blackfriars Bridge its vastness does make the Isle of Dogs seem very close to the City, as it was intended to do. Yet as one gets closer to the building its bulk becomes far less overwhelming.[158]

Cabot Place, East and West (RT1), at the foot of No. 1 Canada Square and extending through to the east end of Cabot Square, provides 9,500 sq.m of retail space (*60*). It

---

[c] The Prime Minister at the time of the opening of the West India Dock in 1802 and after whom the ship which officially opened the dock was named.

63. No. 1 Canada Square (Canary Wharf Tower), looking east across Cabot Square.

includes four levels of shopping, with a glass-domed ro-tunda having a diameter of 26 metres at the east end and Cabot Hall, a public hall with an area of 22,000 sq.m, at the west end. In the middle, the Canary Wharf station on the DLR, where four lines serve six platforms, has an impressive large curved steel-and-glass overall roof, stone-lined walls, and neatly shaped marble benches (*16*). This block was designed by the same team of architects as No. 1 Canada Square, plus Building Design Partnership for the retail elements and A.S.F.A. Limited for the station. The management contractor for the main building was Bovis Construction Ltd, but the construction of the station was separately managed by Mowlem. The building is clad in Indian red sandstone, Briar Hill sandstone from Ohio, and greenstone from the Lake District.[159]

Nos 1 and 7 Westferry Circus and No. 5 West India Avenue (WF3–5 or B1–3) is a linked block, with a curved face to Westferry Circus, and forms the first part of the second phase of the Canary Wharf development (*64*). Olympia & York managed the building contract, and construction work began in 1991. The two Westferry units were designed by Skidmore, Owings & Merrill (principal architects: Robert Turner and David Childs,

respectively) and contain 20,300 sq.m and 14,700 sq.m. They were completed in 1993, and No. 7 is now the UK headquarters of Texaco. The rather box-like Post-Modern block, which is stepped-back and rises to 10 storeys, has a heavy cornice above the fourth floor and a rounded tower at the north-west corner. The building is clad in cream and pinky-brown marbles.

No. 5 West India Avenue was designed by Fred Koetter of Koetter Kim & Associates of Boston, Mass., in conjunction with Perkins & Will. Work on this block stopped after Olympia & York's withdrawal, leaving the completed steel framework as a skeleton. However, work resumed in 1994, and by May 1995 the exterior of the building had been virtually completed.[160] Similar in appearance to Nos 1 and 7 Westferry Circus, it has a 'wrap-around sheath' of sandstone, cream-coloured and with white relieving bands, and will contain 180,000 sq.ft of accommodation.

Nos 17 and 20 Columbus Courtyard (WF6), designed by Aldo Rossi, in association with Perkins & Will, was due to form the final part of the second phase, but in May 1995 no start had been made on the superstructure, although the basement car-parking was decked over.[161]

64. Canary Wharf: Nos 1 and 7 Westferry Circus.

10 *Cannon Workshops*

The Cannon Workshops were built in 1824–5 by the West India Dock Company to the designs of the younger John Rennie as a cooperage surrounded by a quadrangle of workshops and stores buildings (*65*). In 1922–3 the entire group was converted by the PLA to serve as the Central Stores Depot. The south-west corner of the quadrangle had been demolished for road widening in 1893 and the cooperage was destroyed by bombing in 1941, being partly rebuilt in 1957.

The closure of the up-river docks made the Central Stores and works yard redundant. In 1980–1 the PLA set up a project for the refurbishment of the Central Stores, with clearance and redevelopment of the works yard, as an estate of rentable workshops for small businesses, designated 'Cannon Workshops' after a cannon that had stood inside the entrance arch since at least 1914. The development was a joint venture by the PLA and Midland Montague Industrial Leasing, and was organized outside the aegis of the LDDC as part of the PLA's effort to re-

vitalize its redundant property, before there was a broader framework for docklands redevelopment. Regeneration Limited managed the project, the architects for which were Charles Lawrence and David Wrightson. Refurbishment of the old buildings as 72 units was completed by late 1982, and single-storey steel sheds to the south for 45 more units were completed in 1983. The units were let to such diverse tenants as printing firms, architects, barfitters, a jellied-eel producer, Greenpeace, and the Museum in Docklands Project Library and Archive.[162] The conversion of the quadrangle involved doubling the south range with a new inner block, and reconstruction of the bomb-damaged part of the west range. The new sections were given cast-iron columns similar to those surviving on the north range and at either end of the west range. The boarding and lugs were removed from the old columns, and 'loggias' were created in front of aluminium cladding. New doorways were made towards the ends of the south elevation.[163] In 1988 the sheds in the former works yard, which were barely five years old, were cleared

65. Cannon Workshops: aerial view in 1986.

to make way for Westferry Circus. The former stores quadrangle and cooperage survive on the north side of this roundabout, dwarfed by their new neighbours.

12 *City Harbour*

This development occupies a 4.9-acre site on the east side of the Millwall Dock towards its southern end, and adjacent to East Ferry Road. Originally it was known as the Brunel Centre, but the name was changed in 1988. The developers were British Land, the Summit Group (the property and financial services subsidiary of Atlantic Computers), and MBO (a wholly owned subsidiary of the Dutch bank NMB). The architects were Building Design Partnership & Holford Associates, and the main contractor was John Laing Construction.

Work began in 1987 and the first block, Woodchester House (originally known as Lighterman's House), was completed late in 1988. This is a six-storey block providing 36,459 sq.ft of office accommodation. Merchant House, an eight-storey office block, containing 54,962 sq.ft, had been completed by the middle of 1990. The two blocks are ranged around Waterman's Square and have precast-concrete frames, clad in curtain-walling of silver-

grey and shiny-black panels, with reflective, tinted glass. Woodchester House is stepped down towards the quayside, while Merchant House has a more formal and symmetrical main elevation to the dock.

To the east, in Selsdon Way, The Terrace (completed in 1989) is a two- to seven-storey office block, offset in two parts, in yellow stock-type brick, with some rendering (part incised) and glazed curtain-walling. There are balconies with metal railings, and the roof is flat, although there is a series of gables along the front elevation. There are seven office units, varying in size from 13,530 sq.ft to 4,420 sq.ft. This block also incorporates a public multi-storey car park, which to the rear (east) elevation is more high-tech in appearance, with slatted panels and an external, metal-braced framework.

Plans to build a further office block (City Harbour House, to complete Waterman's Square) and a dockside 20-storey hotel, had not been implemented by May 1995.[164]

Docklands Sailing Centre, Westferry Road   19

Situated at the west end of the Millwall Outer Dock, the centre was built in 1988–9 (*66*). In 1987 the LDDC

66. Docklands Sailing Centre, Millwall Docks, looking north-west.

sponsored a limited architectural competition for the design of a new centre to serve the needs of water sports
such as sailing, windsurfing, angling and canoeing. A fast-
track design-and-build contract had already been agreed
with John Laing Construction and the winning design
had to be implementable in this way. The competition
was won by Kit Allsopp Architects. The LDDC provided
funding of £1.3 million, and the Sports Council a further
£200,000. The centre is run by a trust on which the
LDDC, Tower Hamlets Borough Council and local
groups are represented.

The presence of old dock walls below ground made it
virtually impossible to build the centre across the middle
of the site and it was therefore placed right against
Westferry Road, where there is a high brick boundary
wall. The building is basically a two-storey 'pavilion',
with changing rooms, manager's office, teaching areas,
equipment store, workshop and plant at ground-floor
level, and lounge, bar, members' room, kitchen, crèche
and offices on the first floor. To the dockside, a balcony
of wood and steel, with an external staircase, runs along
the entire length of the upper floor. The ground floor is
clad in yellow stock brick, while the first floor is faced in
timber-framed glass and infill panels. The large pitched
roof is timber-trussed and partially translucent, with an
overhang, to cover the entrance area, boat-store and

workshops. Such a roof is a favourite device of the architects and in this case derives from their structure designed for the Stoke Garden Festival in 1986. Overall,
colour was deliberately kept to a minimum, the natural
tones and textures of the materials being retained.[165]

Dollar Bay

See The Business Centre, Dollar Bay, page 53.

East India Dock Site   20

This 5.9-acre site on the south-west side of the dock represented the second phase of the redevelopment of the
East India Import Dock (the first being the *Financial
Times* and Telehouse Europe buildings) (*67*). It was developed by Nordic Construction Company, a Swedish
real-estate and construction group, with funding from
Trygg Hansa SPP, a large Swedish insurance and pension
company, and to designs by Sten Samuelson of Malmö,
and the British-based Beaton Thomas Partnership. Work
began in September 1989 and was completed in 1992.
Birse Construction was the main contractor for the foundations, basements and structural frame, at a cost of
£21.3 million, while the cladding contract, worth over
£20 million, was carried out by Hinchliffe Façades.

67. East India Dock development, looking west along the canal to Lighterman's House.

68. East India Dock development: the 'Domino Players', a sculpture by Kim Bennett.

Enterprise Business Park

The business park, on the south side of Marsh Wall and between its junctions with Millharbour and Mastmaker Road, was one of the first commercial developments in the newly designated Enterprise Zone. The 5.5-acre site was developed and constructed by Wimpey, using a scheme designed by Newman Levinson & Partners, with flexible units of between 5,200 sq.ft and 20,000 sq.ft, for industrial and commercial use (with office provision).

The first phase, in 1983–5, cost a reported £1.9 million, and consists of three two-storey 'pavilions', each supported on a single central column, allowing flexible internal subdivision. The faceted exterior has polyester-coated, buff-coloured cladding panels, fixed to exposed, brightly coloured metal frames. On the upper storey are high-tech oriel windows, and individual units are identified with large cut-out lettering (*69*).[167]

The *Guardian* newspaper acquired the ownership of the second phase for a new printing works, and Wimpey managed construction of the building (1985–7), at a reported cost of £14 million. It is a rectangular box of 6,000 sq.m, and the architects sought to minimize the bulk of the building by using tinted glass and reflective panels of silver-blue colour, blurring the distinction between solid and sky. The long elevations are broken into bays by red porticos, while bold horizontal louvres help to make the press hall seem less tall. An Art-Deco-style tower at one corner is topped by a mast bearing the newspaper's name (*52*).[168]

Exchange Square

See Harbour Exchange, page 73.

Financial Times Printing Works, No. 240 East India Dock Road

This is one of the most generally acclaimed modern buildings in Docklands and has received a number of awards and commendations.[169] The building, which had to be ready within a year to house two new printing presses already on order, was designed by Nicholas Grimshaw & Partners, with Robinson Design Partnership, who, as specialists in the design of printing works, were responsible for most of the interior layout and fitting. The management contractor was Bovis, and the cost of construction was £18 million. Clearance of the five-acre site began early in 1987, piling started in April, and the building was operational in September 1988.[170]

The steel-framed, flat-roofed building was designed not only to be erected quickly but also to allow flexibility in its future use. The plan is very simple, with a long press hall to the north, offices on three floors to the south, a spinal plant room running east-west between these two, a paper store at one end of the building, and a despatch bay at the other. The most notable features are the specially designed screens which run along most of the north and south elevations. That to East India Dock

The four linked blocks of five to ten storeys (plus basement car parks) are in a monumental Post-Modern style, with colonnades, arches and gridded windows, including multi-storey bays. They are faced in pink Sardinian granite, Rosa Limbara Chiandonato, and have hipped and pitched roofs, covered with pantile-type roofing sheets. Three of the blocks have a full-height landscaped atrium. The development comprises 600,000 sq.ft of office accommodation, together with provision for shops, restaurant, wine bar and recreational facilities.

Lighterman's House (No. 3 Clove Crescent), at the south-west corner of the development, is curved to take account of the quadrant-shaped site, which is partly bounded by the historic East India Dock wall. Part of the inner curve of this block closes the main vista, which consists of one arm of an L-shaped canal, lined by trees, crossed by humped, metal footbridges, and containing fountains. Another canal runs along the northern side of the development. At the north-western corner is Mulberry Place (No. 5 Clove Crescent, since 1993 occupied by Tower Hamlets Borough Council Central Services), while the other two blocks, Nos 1 and 2 Clove Crescent, are to the east. Set around the site are a number of open-air sculptures all executed in 1992, including 'Renaissance' (bronze) by Maurice Blik, 'Meridian Metaphor' (granite) by David Jacobson, 'Domino Players' (bronze) by Kim Bennett (*68*), and 'Shadow Play' (steel and bronze) by Dave King.[166]

69. Enterprise Business Park: No. 2 Millharbour, looking north-west towards the towers of
South Quay Waterside and Canary Wharf.

70. The *Financial Times* Printing Works, No. 240 East India Dock Road, north front looking west at night.

Road is 96m by 16m, formed with two-square-metre panes of clear glass. The panes are bolted to stainless-steel plates, hung from tie rods which run up and over the tops of columns placed every six metres. Projecting steel arms cantilevered out horizontally from the columns hold the panes of glass in place. All this allows the inside of the screen to be completely flush, without any internal projections, and permits passing motorists to see the printing presses in action (70). A similar screen is provided on the south elevation, but, with office accommodation behind, the glass panes are tinted; at the centre of this elevation are two aluminium-clad, half-rounded, projecting towers, set closely together and housing lifts and stairs; the main entrance to the building is squeezed insignificantly between the towers. The two ends of the building, with rounded corners, are also clad in grey aluminium.

In the spring of 1995 it was announced that the *Financial Times* intended to transfer its printing operation to West Ferry Printers (see page 86) and close down the East India Dock Road premises.[171] Thus, the future of one of the finest buildings in Docklands is uncertain.

Fleet House

See The Mansion, page 79.

Glengall Bridge

26

This development, providing 350,000 sq.ft of residential, commercial and retail space, stretches across the Millwall Dock from Crossharbour to Millharbour. It was developed by Glengall Bridge Ltd, a company specially formed for the purpose by a combination of London and Edinburgh Trust, Balfour Beatty Developments and Warleggan Estates, and was designed by Richard Seifert & Partners. The eastern and western halves of the scheme were developed as separate phases.

The £27-million contract for the first half was awarded to Balfour Beatty in 1987 and was completed in 1989.

71. Glengall Bridge West, view from the east across the lifting bridge spanning the Millwall Docks.

72. Glengall Bridge West, the quadrant colonnade at Millharbour.

Aegon House (originally to be called St Andrew's House and known for a time as Regency House) is an eight-storey office block, flanked by two more four-storey office blocks – Balmoral and Melrose Houses. A three-storey range (with four-storey pavilions) of 'versatile business units' runs from the corner of Balmoral House and has an arcaded ground floor with squat columns, in a style copied from some of the more monumental early dock warehouses. Its Z-plan allows a parade of shops along Pepper Street, a courtyard to the rear (Lanark Square), and a quayside area (Turnberry Quay). The housing is massed beside the dock in a block varying between four and six storeys, with a large archway providing access through the building to the two-leaf lifting-bridge specially built to connect the two halves of the scheme across the dock. The accommodation consists of 16 one- and two-bedroom flats, and two three-bedroom houses. The eastern half of Glengall Bridge is completed by a two-storey polygonal pavilion, with a steeply pitched hipped roof, which since completion has been a wine bar.

Construction of the second phase, Glengall Bridge West, was carried out by Mowlem Management in 1989–91 at a cost of £28 million (71, 72). It consists of 11 blocks in similar materials to the first part, and ranging from three to eight storeys, providing a total of 210,000 sq.ft of office and retail space, plus a proposed waterside restaurant.[172]

Great Eastern Enterprise

This stands on a 4.5-acre site on the east side of Millharbour and was developed in three phases in 1984–9 by Standard Commercial Property Securities, the property

29

73. Great Eastern Enterprise, on the west side of Millwall Docks: the low-rise first phase built in the mid-1980s.

subsidiary of the brewers Bass.[173] The early sketches were prepared by Howell Killick Partridge & Amis, who established the broad design philosophy, but the developer used a design-and-build contract, in conjunction with D. J. Curtis & Associates, a Leeds architectural firm.[174]

The first phase, costing about £2.4 million,[175] consists of four two-storey blocks, intended as a mixture of workshops and offices, but all, in fact, initially let as offices.[176] The buildings are clad in powder-coated green aluminium curtain-walling and tinted glazing, with green glazing-bars. There are red-brick plinths and white steel stairs (*73*).[177]

In 1986 the scheme was extended to an adjacent site,[178] where a five-storey block with 29,243 sq.ft was taken as offices by the Builder publishing group, which moved into the block in March 1989.[179] The final office block, Great Eastern House, has six storeys and contains 42,450 sq.ft. It was acquired by the Midland Bank. These last two blocks were constructed by J. & J. Fee of Halifax for £10 million.[180]

30 *Greenwich View*

At the southern end of Millharbour and on the edge of the Millwall Outer Dock, this was another development,

here exclusively of offices, by Robert Ogden/Indescon Developments Ltd, following the success of their Indescon Court project (see page 77). Like Indescon Court, the scheme was designed by Richard Seifert & Partners, and Indescon was again the main contractor. A low-rise phase (1985–8) of five two- and three-storey high-tech blocks, very similar to Indescon Court, was followed by a high-rise phase (1988–90), known as City Reach and comprising two nine-storey blocks (City Reach One and West Tower), with a shared four-storey atrium, and faced in polished granite and black reflective glazed curtain-walling (*74*). In addition, Pointe North (1988–90) is a four-storey building, clad with white panels and black reflective glazed curtain-walling, entirely constructed over water, with its own moorings.[181]

Harbour Exchange 31

Occupying Exchange Square, at the corner of Marsh Wall and Limeharbour, this is a large and complex development, comprising a series of blocks built in phases (*13, 48*). It involved four architectural firms and several developers, although the overall concept was provided by Trevor Davison of the Property Design Group, and Charter Group Developments acted as the 'lead developer'.

74. Greenwich View, Millwall Docks: City Reach One and West Tower.

The original 3.5-hectare site was previously occupied by the former No. 1 Olsen Shed on the Millwall Dock, which had only been refurbished and extended in 1984 by Maskell Warehousing, at a cost of £7 million. Nevertheless, in 1986 the site, partly owned by Maskells and partly by the LDDC, was acquired by a relocation-design company based in Milton Keynes and headed by Simon Miller, which was then known as the Interdec Design Group, but which was subsequently renamed the Charter Group. Additional adjoining land was purchased to extend the site eventually to ten acres and arrangements were made with the LDDC to buy its West India Dock House and a section of the Millwall Dock. Miller and architects Sheppard Robson drew up a master-plan for the site comprising a series of self-contained office blocks for development by intending occupiers and involving the demolition of the existing warehouse. The Charter Group invited AMEC (formed by the merger of Fairclough Construction and Press Engineering) to join in the development of part of the site and to provide design-and-build schemes for the other phases. Charter Group developed the infrastructure and communal facilities. Part of the funding for the whole project came from a syndicate led by the Japanese Sanwa Bank, which provided a £60-million facility.[182] In the event, the Charter Group was involved in the development of every phase of Harbour Exchange.

The sequence of developments on the site was as follows:

No. 3 Exchange Square (1987–8) is an 11-storey block providing 92,000 sq.ft of offices. The developers were Charter Group and AMEC, the architects Sheppard

Robson and the main contractor Fairclough. The cost was approximately £1 million.

Exchange Tower (Nos 1 and 2 Exchange Square) (1987–8) is a pair of 18-storey blocks (effectively one building). The developer was Charter Group, the architects Frederick Gibberd Coombes & Partners and the main contractor Fairclough. At 32,000 sq.m, it was said to have the largest continuous curtain-walling in Europe.[183] (Nos 2 and 3 Exchange Square were purchased by the Eighth Property Enterprise Trust.)[184]

Nos 6 and 7 Exchange Square (1987–9) are eight- and ten-storey blocks, providing 129,000 sq.ft of accommodation. The developers were Charter Group and A. F. Budge, a Nottinghamshire-based construction and mining company,[185] the architects were Frederick Gibberd Coombes & Partners and the main contractor was Alfred McAlpine. The cost was £14.7 million.[186]

Harbour Island (Nos 10–39, Exchange Square) (1987–8) is constructed on piled foundations over the water in the Millwall Dock. A three-storey block of shops, with offices above, and a public house in the centre, it gives a total of 68,000 sq.ft of accommodation. The developers were Charter Group and Berkeley House Properties, the architects were Haverstock Associates and the main contractors Fairclough Howard Marine and Multi Construction (Southern) Ltd. The cost was £9.7 million.[187] This phase was purchased in 1987 by the Laser 1988 Trust (see page 51).[188] One unusual feature of the Harbour Island building is that the curtain-walling has timber rather than aluminium frames. These were

75. Heron Quays looking north-east.

manufactured by Devizes Joinery, using Iroko, a very durable African hardwood.[189] The public house in the centre of Harbour Island, the Spinnaker (No. 19 Exchange Square), was fitted out at a cost of £500,000 by Greene King, the brewers, and was opened in May 1989.[190]

Nos 4 and 5 Exchange Square (1987–8) are two blocks, of five to eight storeys, containing 55,000 sq.ft and 38,000 sq.ft of office accommodation. The developers were Charter Group and Higgs & Hills Developments, in association with London & Metropolitan, the architects were Sheppard Robson and the main contractor Fairclough Building.[191]

Nos 8 and 9 Exchange Square (1988–90) provide 7,750 sq.m and 5,810 sq.m of office accommodation in eight- and ten-storey blocks. The developer was Charter Group, the architects were Frederick Gibberd Coombes & Partners and the main contractor was Alfred McAlpine. The cost was £16 million. Late in 1988 Nos 8 and 9 were purchased by Sheraton Securities for £36 million.[192] However, in March 1991 this property went into receivership.[193]

Apart from Harbour Island, the blocks are of reinforced-concrete construction, using fast-track methods, with silver and blue reflective-glass curtain-walling, and bases clad in mottled green marble. As a centrepiece to Exchange Square, a bronze sculpture, 'Wind of Change', depicting larger-than-life rowing-men and women in

boats, was specially commissioned from André Wallace by the developers, Charter Group Developments, at a cost of £40,000. Situated outside the west elevation of Exchange Tower, on a raised landscaped area, it was unveiled in September 1990.[194] Two electric cranes by Stothert & Pitt, dating from the 1960s, and used at the Millwall Docks, are now preserved as 'features' on the west side of Exchange Square, alongside Harbour Island.[195]

Harbour Quay, Wood Wharf Business Park   32

A development on a 1.5-acre site towards the north-east corner of the central dock of the West India Docks, this consists of two steel-framed high-tech pavilions, intended for office and warehouse use. The developers were Standard Commercial Property Securities (the property development group of the brewers Bass), in association with Port of London Properties, and construction was carried out in 1986–7. The two blocks provide a total of 45,000 sq.ft of accommodation.[196]

Heron Quays   33

The existing development at Heron Quays, to the south of Canary Wharf and running eastwards off Marsh Wall, was part of a much larger scheme intended to cover the whole of the eight-acre site. This scheme, first commissioned in 1981, was designed by Nicholas Lacey, Jobst & Hyett, for the developers, Tarmac Brookglade Properties Ltd. It was designed in five sections, each centred around an open space, and was intended to contain a mixture of uses: office, retail, residential, light industrial and business – with the residential to be built last, on the easternmost end of the quay.[197] By 1995 only two phases, with Tarmac acting as its own contractor, had been constructed (in 1984–9), providing 170,000 sq.ft of office space, and they have been generally well received.[198]

The built phases consist of a series of high-tech 'cabins' or 'Swiss chalets', with light steel structures, covered with red, purple and blue-grey vitreous enamel panels, while the monopitch roofs are clad in aluminium (56, 75). The corners of the blocks are enlivened by white-painted steel balconies. Because of the historically important nineteenth-century underwater dock wall, the weight of the new buildings had to be kept six metres away from the edge of the quay. Steel piers were, therefore, driven into the water and steel cross-beams, left exposed, were laid on top of them to carry the weight of the buildings and allow them to project over the water, giving extra space at no additional land cost.[199]

A number of proposals have subsequently been put forward for the development of the rest of the site and for redeveloping the existing buildings. In particular, in 1988 David Gosling, Stephen Proctor and John Ferguson were appointed by the LDDC to prepare a master-plan for the redevelopment of Heron Quays, to take account of its proximity to Canary Wharf. However, nothing further has been built on the site, nor have proposals to rebuild the existing low-rise phase been implemented.[200]

Hertsmere House

This is situated off Marsh Wall, at the north-west corner of the West India Import Dock. The building was begun as a speculative venture by the Hertsmere Group, but was sold in 1986 to Hilstone Developments, who in 1987 sold it on to Mountleigh for £12 million. It was designed by Newman Levinson & Partners, with construction by Mowlem (1987–8). The four-storey red-brick building has an arcaded ground floor to the quayside, intended to echo the nearby warehouses on North Quay; inside there is a three-storey marble-clad atrium.[201]

34

76. The Innovation Centre, No. 225 Marsh Wall.

36 Indescon Court

This was built during 1982–3 on a 4.4-acre site at the junction of Millharbour and Lighterman's Road. It was designed by Richard Seifert & Partners for the Indescon Group, a Darlington-based firm, which sold the whole development project for £3.5 million to Robert Ogden Estates, an Otley property developer. A subsidiary of Indescon, IBS Construction, acted as the main contractor. A range of medium-sized, steel-framed, modular buildings, set around a landscaped courtyard, provides 12 factories and warehouses (with offices). They are covered in white-metal cladding, broken by blue, reflective, glazed curtain-walling, while the double-rise hipped roofing incorporates mansard glazing. In all, it provides 70,465 sq.ft of factory and warehouse space and 16,885 sq.ft of offices.[202]

37 Innovation Centre, No. 225 Marsh Wall

The Innovation Centre was developed and built by William Sindall, with funding from the Carroll Group, and designed by Fielden & Mawson (76). Construction

was carried out between 1989 and 1992, at a cost of £15 million. The four-storey centre – intended as a second-generation version of the Cambridge Science Park – has an atrium, paved with polished Purbeck stone, around which high-tech research-and-development suites are arranged, as well as conference and meeting facilities. The suites have heavy floor-loading capacities, are connected for three-phase electricity, and have fibre-optic links to nearby satellite stations. The reinforced-concrete-framed block has a suitably high-tech exterior, with silver panels and black-glass curtain-walling, and a vestigial pediment to the Marsh Wall elevation.[203]

38 Isle of Dogs Neighbourhood Centre, Jack Dash House, Marsh Wall

The building provides 45,000 sq.ft of accommodation on a 0.6-acre site, and was erected by the LDDC for the Isle of Dogs Neighbourhood of the Borough of Tower Hamlets, in return for land at Poplar Dock owned by Tower Hamlets and required for new roadworks. The Neighbourhood Council commissioned Florian Beigel to design the centre, but the LDDC insisted on holding a

77. Isle of Dogs Neighbourhood Centre, Jack Dash House, Marsh Wall.

limited architectural competition, which was won by Chassay Architects of Paddington (Tchaik Chassay and Malcolm Last) with an accomplished design in the currently fashionable 1930s-Modern style. Construction was carried out in 1989–91 by J. A. Elliott Ltd – who won a further competition for the design-and-build contract – at a cost of £4 million, and the building opened in February 1992. The two linked blocks are set at right-angles on two sides of a grassed courtyard and provide respectively for administrative and community functions (77). These buildings are white-rendered, with light-buff brick and glazed curtain-walling, the taller five-storey office block to Marsh Wall having a curved roof. At the south-east corner a two-storey rotunda or tower, clad in light-buff brick, has an exhibition area below and a council chamber, approached by an external curved staircase, above. The building is named after the dockers' leader who was active in the London docks in the 1950s and 1960s.[204]

Jack Dash House

See Isle of Dogs Neighbourhood Centre, above.

The Ladkarn Building (re-sited)

This was situated on a 0.45-hectare site on the east side of the West India Dock, between the northern and central docks, that was leased from the PLA. It was commissioned by Ladkarn Haulage, a firm involved in earth-moving, the hire of plant, and civil-engineering sub-contracting. Nicholas Grimshaw & Partners (project architect David Harriss) produced an outline design for a flexibly planned building, providing offices and a large repair workshop. Erection was carried out by Ladkarn themselves, in about seven months during 1985.

The building, with rounded corners, had a shiny silver cladding with a horizontal blue stripe, and was supported by a bright-red external steel frame (54). It had a total

78. Limehouse Studios, West India Docks: a television production set for 'Network 7' in 1988.

area of 1,552 sq.m. As soon as the building was completed it became evident that it would have to make way for the Canary Wharf development, and the architects, with such a possibility in mind, had designed the Ladkarn Building to be movable. It was dismantled and re-erected in Alpine Way, Beckton, during 1987–8.[205]

The Lanterns 41

Built on a three-acre site off the west side of Millharbour, this was developed and erected in 1983–4 by Multi Construction Developments, part of the A. Roberts Group (47). The 44 single-storey units are arranged in straight rows, around a courtyard, with an additional two-storey office block at the entrance from Millharbour. The accommodation totals 51,000 sq.ft, with individual units ranging from 500 sq.ft to 3,200 sq.ft.[206]

Limeharbour Court 42

This stands on the east side of Limeharbour. It is a five-storey (plus basement) block, providing 26,636 sq.ft of office accommodation. It was developed by Tweed Finance Ltd in conjunction with Charter Group Developments, and was completed in April 1989. The flat-roofed building is clad in black-tinted, glazed curtain-walling and red brick.[207]

Limehouse Studios (demolished)

These studios were created within No. 30 Shed on the South Quay of the West India Import Dock (7). This was one of two two-storey warehouses built there by John Mowlem & Company to the designs of W. P. Sheppard-Baron. Completed in 1954, they had reinforced-concrete frames, floors and slab roofs and brick wall panels.[208]

In 1982–3 it was converted as the country's largest independent television production studios, for Limehouse Productions, a firm set up to coincide with the launch of Channel 4, and in anticipation of growth in video, cable and satellite television. The warehouse was acquired through the LDDC, to which it had passed in 1981, and the conversion of its eastern half as Limehouse Studios was by Laing Management Contracting, to designs by the Terry Farrell Partnership, for £3,680,460. The removal of floors and columns permitted the formation of two large and elaborately equipped studios (78). The north side of the building was adapted to form a reception area, control rooms, offices and dressing-rooms.[209] The austerity and scale of the warehouse exterior was broken down by the superimposition of a Post-Modern façade, of 'little buildings climbing over a massive building like Lilliputians climbing over Gulliver',[210] made of blue and black enamelled-steel cladding panels on a ceramic plinth. Six abstract bird shapes symbolized 'the waterside location and the spirit of communication'.[211] The establishment of Limehouse Studios in the early days of the Enterprise Zone was considered an important step in the regeneration of Docklands, and indeed for a short time this was a shining example of the profitable conversion of a dockside building. However, from 1985 Limehouse Studios was overshadowed by the Canary Wharf scheme. The premises were sold to Olympia & York for £25 million in 1988, and the building was demolished in 1989.[212]

43 *Littlejohn Frazer, No. 1 Park Place (formerly No. 2 Canary Wharf)*

This is a freehold office block, perched at the south-western corner of Canary Wharf, which was developed by a City accountants' firm as their own headquarters (*51*). It was designed by Stanley Trevor and constructed in 1985–7 by Trollope & Colls. The cost of development was believed to have been in excess of £3.2 million. It consists of two linked polygonal blocks, of four and six storeys (including attics), faced in yellowish brown brick, with mansard roofs.[213]

45 *London Arena*

This was created in 1984–6 by the conversion of K Shed (Olsen Shed 2), one of a pair of sheds built at the Millwall Docks in 1969 by John Mowlem & Company for Fred Olsen Lines' Canary Islands trade (*48*). Olsen Lines left the Millwall Docks in 1976 and the shed was then used by the PLA until 1980.

From 1982 Lord Selsdon, Chairman of the Greater London and South East Regional Council for Sport and Recreation, and the sports promoter and commentator Ron Pickering fostered the establishment of 'the U.K.'s largest' indoor sports and leisure complex, with support from the LDDC, which gave the site at a peppercorn rent. The conversion, scheduled to cost £8 million, was funded partly by a consortium of Bovis, GEC and Mecca Entertainment, and partly by the LDDC, the Sports Council, the Amateur Athletics Association and Tower Hamlets Borough Council. Bovis were the management contractors. The facility was opened in March 1986.[214] However, the original plans had been superseded by a more ambitious scheme, planned in 1985 and carried out in 1987–9. The final cost of the whole conversion was £24 million. To improve commercial viability the building was adapted for international boxing and major concerts, with Frank Warren and Harvey Goldsmith brought in as additional promoters. This involved replacement of the central bays with a tall new structure to seat 12,615. The architects were Stewart K. Riddick & Partners. The steel frame was designed by Fairhursts and assembled by Graham Wood. The main hall is an enormous hangar-like building with an uninterrupted span of 281ft (86m) on 59ft (18m) columns, the largest such hall erected in Britain since the Wembley Arena of 1934. Parts of the 1969 shed survive at the south end, the administration area, and in the North Hall (the sports complex). The London Arena went into receivership in 1991, but in 1994 it was sold to the Spectator Management Group, an American company based in Philadelphia, which already managed the Sheffield Arena. This company has initiated a programme of sporting events and entertainment aimed at reviving the London Arena's fortunes.[215]

London Telehouse

See The Telehouse Europe, page 83.

48 *McDonald's Drive-Thru Restaurant, Trafalgar Way*

This stands between Trafalgar Way and Aspen Way (*79*). It was designed by Assael Architecture for McDonald's Restaurants Ltd, and the main contractors were Walkers. It opened in December 1994.[216]

79. McDonald's Drive-Thru Restaurant, Trafalgar Way.

50 *The Mansion, No. 197 Marsh Wall (formerly Fleet House)*

This is a five-storey office block providing 43,000 sq.ft of accommodation, with a basement car park. It was developed by the National Leasing & Finance Company, and was designed by Seifert Ltd, who also managed the fast-track building contract. Work began about the middle of 1988 and was completed by the summer of 1989. The block is clad in polished flame-green and two shades of grey granite; each elevation has a central pedimented gable, and the front elevation has a pedimented entrance.[217]

51 *Nos 30 and 40 Marsh Wall*

These are two six-storey office blocks developed by Charter Developments, who were also responsible for Harbour Exchange. In all, its 92,000 sq.ft of space provide for 47 office suites ranging in size from 500 sq.ft to 4,500 sq.ft. Construction (1990–2) of the £34-million scheme was begun by Elliott of Bishop's Stortford, but, after they went into receivership in February 1991, the work was completed by Team.[218]

53 *Mastmaker Court, Nos 20–34 (even) Mastmaker Road*

This is a development by Pirin Ltd, completed in 1987. The two blocks of blue-and-beige, pitched-roofed 'shiny sheds' are divided into a total of eight light industrial and office units, providing about 57,000 sq.ft of accommodation.[219]

54 *Mercury Earth Satellite Station and Telecommunications Centre, East Wood Wharf*

In 1984 Marconi of Chelmsford constructed and erected two dish aerials on PLA-owned land, for Mercury Communications, to provide an earth satellite station, giving voice and data transatlantic communication, particularly between New York and London. Subsequently a telecommunications centre was added (opened in 1989) to house the British end of Mercury's fibre-optics cable to France and the equipment for their three earth stations linked with North America and Europe.[220]

55 *Meridian Gate*

This office development stands to the north of Marsh Wall, overlooking the South Dock of the West India Docks. A £50-million scheme was designed for the COR-DOR Group, a Kuwaiti consortium, by SSC Consultants of Bristol, to be implemented in phases on the 3.8-acre site.

The first phase, providing 45,000 sq.ft of office space, consists of two linked blocks of four and five storeys: Malvern and Polden Houses, and Brecon, Cairngorm, and Grampian Houses. They were built within 13 months in 1987–8, under a £3.5-million fast-track contract, by Try Construction. The steel-framed structures are faced in red brick, with large expanses of curtain-walling.

The second phase comprises Snowdon, Moorfoot, Intourist, Cumbrian, Memaco and Quantock Houses, arranged in two U-plan ranges around a central courtyard. They were constructed in 1987–9 by John Laing, at an estimated £7 million. In all they gave a further 70,000 sq.ft of office space, together with provision for a quayside restaurant. More high-tech in appearance, the blocks are faced in yellow brick, tinted blue glass, and light-cream panels (*80*), and each range has a central entrance-porch from the courtyard, with a heavy Post-Modern split-pediment and rounded pillars, all of which are in dark red.[221]

The third phase, planned to consist of two large office blocks and commence construction in 1988, was redesigned – in the light of the changing property market – as six smaller units, but by May 1995 no work had commenced on site.[222]

80. Meridian Gate, Marsh Wall: the north (dockside) elevations of Cumbrian, Memaco and Quantock Houses *(left to right)*.

56 *Milltech*

Erected on the east side of Millharbour in 1984, this development was designed by the John Brunton Partnership as a 13,000-sq.ft high-tech factory unit, with ancillary offices. The project was begun by College Hill Securities and Geoffrey Osborne, but was taken over and completed by Paul Sykes Developments. The building was occupied by Pritchard Services, who arranged for a first floor to be built over the production space, creating a total of 17,850 sq.ft of office space. It is a two-storey 'shiny shed', with silver corrugated cladding and mirrored glass. A low-pitched roof rises to a central ridge.[223]

57 *Millwall Park Centre and Club*

The Millwall Park Centre and One O'Clock Club building was erected in 1992 on the west side of Stebondale Street on a plot of land in the north-east corner of Millwall Park. The two-storey structure was designed as a sports and social club and children's play centre by Avanti Architects. The chief contractor was R. Mansell and the cost was £562,342.[224]

58 *Mowlem Site, Nos 52–58 (even) Marsh Wall*

This triangular plot on the south side of the road, west of Mastmaker Road, was developed by Mowlem, the construction and engineering firm, which between 1923 and 1976 held the contract for civil engineering and building maintenance throughout the PLA estate. From the 1930s Mowlem had a site on the south side of Marsh Wall, immediately to the east of what is now No. 50, using it for storage and site offices; one of the sheds remained there until the mid-1980s. Mowlem was able to acquire the one-acre site from the LDDC in 1984, and two three-storey blocks (Nos 52 & 54 and Nos 56 & 58 Marsh Wall) were designed and built by the firm, being completed in 1986. Initially, No. 58 was used by Mowlem as a regional office, while No. 54 was taken by the National Westminster Bank as its Docklands branch. The buildings have partly curved faces and are mainly clad in silver panels, with black-tinted glass.[225]

59 *Former Northern and Shell Building, No. 41a Millharbour*

This was developed by Northern and Shell, the international publishing group, as their own headquarters building. It was designed by Stanley Trevor, and constructed by A. Roberts in 1983–4. The three-storey block in traditional brickwork-construction, with bronze-finished windows, provides 18,000 sq.ft of office space. Northern and Shell moved to City Harbour in June 1993 (see page 66).[226]

61 *Passmore Building, Mastmaker Road*

The building is a silver and blue 'shiny shed' with 34,000 sq.ft of accommodation. It was built in 1983–4 on the 1.6-acre site by Richard Passmore, a builder's merchant previously in Limehouse, as the firm's own headquarters and manufacturing plant. The development contract was valued at approximately £1 million. It was empty by 1991 and remained so in May 1995, although a refurbishment of the building was then nearing completion.[227]

62 *PDX Building, Millharbour*

This is an 11,600-sq.ft building designed by the Geoffrey Thorpe Practice for PDX, a printing and office-supply company, as the latter's own headquarters. It was completed by 1985. The building is a flat-roofed 'shiny shed', faced partly in silver and blue corrugated cladding, with blue retaining strips and a red-brick plinth, and partly with mirrored and tinted glazing.[228]

64 *Poplar Business Park*

A four-acre site on the west side of Preston's Road, just south of Poplar High Street, this was developed by Port of London Properties Ltd to replace the 56 units of phases 2 and 3 of Cannon Workshops, demolished to make way for the Canary Wharf scheme. The Canary Wharf Development Company agreed to pay all the relocation costs of those displaced tenants who wished to move to the new site. Designed by YRM (Yorke, Rosenberg & Mardall), construction was carried out in 1987–8 by Canary Wharf Contractors (a consortium of Sir Robert McAlpine, Laing, Mowlem, Costain and Taylor Woodrow). It consists of one two-storey and two single-storey blocks, containing 60 offices and workshops, ranging in size from 680 sq.ft to 1,540 sq.ft. They are clad in light-grey panels, with dark-grey doors and frames, and tinted glazing. The hipped roofs are covered with corrugated cladding.[229]

66 *Price Waterhouse Building, No. 161 Marsh Wall*

Standing on Island Quay, at the south-west corner of the West India Docks, the building was designed by Swedish architects, Sten Samuelsson and Klas Nilsson, for the British subsidiaries of two leading Swedish developers, ABV International and Fabege Property. It was originally conceived as a Scandinavian Trade Centre, with office space for Scandinavian and British 'high technology and financial industries', as well as an exhibition atrium. The building was erected in 1986–8, at an estimated cost of £10 million, with the piling and foundations by Peter Birse and the superstructure by Small Construction (design work for the latter contract was by Tony Gee & Partners). In the event, the building was let in its entirety to the accountants Price Waterhouse. The five-storey high-tech block stands on 110 piles and has a superstructure of framed steelwork and lightweight composite-concrete floors, cast on steel decking. It is clad in shiny white panels and dark glass, intended to reflect and highlight the waterside setting (53).[230]

67 Quay View

This is a three-storey, yellow-brick block on the south side of the Millwall Docks, just outside the Enterprise Zone. It was developed by Trafalgar House as an adjunct to its Timber Wharves housing scheme and was completed in December 1988. It contains eight office units, providing a total of 16,000 sq.ft.[231]

69 Reuters Docklands Centre

Completed in June 1989, the centre straddles a former Victorian dry dock at Blackwall Yard. The Richard Rogers Partnership designed the exterior and core of this international data-processing centre, while specialists Fitzroy Robinson were employed to design and oversee the fitting out and internal layout. The total cost, including fitting out, was £85 million. The 27,900-sq.m building is a typical Richard Rogers high-tech design, less exuberant than his Lloyd's Building, although splashes of colour are provided by the bright-green ducts, yellow cleaning-cranes and blue fire escapes (81). The solid and glazed cladding panels are designed to be interchangeable to allow the rearrangement of office and data floors.[232]

82. Skylines, Limeharbour, north-west corner of the courtyard.

81. Reuters Docklands Centre, Blackwall Yard, view looking west.

Scandinavian Trade Centre

See Price Waterhouse Building, page 81.

70 Skylines

Standing at the junction of Marsh Wall and Limeharbour, this is a low-rise high-tech group of office units, intended to be owner-occupied. It was jointly developed by John Laing and the London Industrial Association, and was designed by Hutchinson Partners, Libby & Company. Construction was carried out by Laings in 1984–6, at a cost of £3.8 million. Originally planned as 41 units, with sizes ranging from 60 sq.m to 418 sq.m, between 1986 and 1988 the number seems to have varied between 36 and 40 units.

A series of blocks, ranging from one to four storeys, is partly arranged along the street frontages to emphasize the street pattern, and partly in blocks to the rear, to form informal courtyard areas (82). The buildings are in brick, with large, stepped, basically triangular red aluminium-framed window-grids, braced with hubs and spokes, and pitched or monopitched roofs, covered with white cladding which in places also runs down the upper parts of the walls. The shapes consciously echo the cranes and sails of the old docks, while the lively roofscape was intended to be seen from the Docklands Light Railway – then planned but not built. Each office unit was given its own front door, with a triangular porch canopy, concrete cannonball, and 'cheese sandwich'.

A second phase of 18 more office units, Skylines Two, was built by Laings in 1988–90. The design of the buildings is very similar to the original part, although the architects were Sidney Kaye Firmin, but the accommodation was greater, with floor areas of between 1,060 sq.ft and 2,450 sq.ft.[233]

South Quay Plaza, Marsh Wall   71

This stands on a five-acre site on the south side of the South West India Dock, previously occupied by Shed 19, a three-storey concrete warehouse built in 1965 to handle Far East cargo. The joint developers were Marples International and National Leasing & Finance, while the scheme was designed by Richard Seifert & Partners, and constructed by Marples. The seven-storey Peterborough Court was built in 1985–7. Containing 103,710 sq.ft of accommodation, it was begun as a speculative office

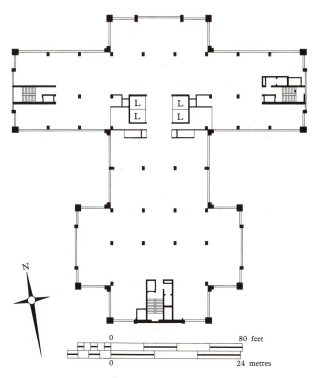

83. South Quay Plaza 2 office block, a typical floor-plan.

block, but was acquired during construction by the *Daily Telegraph* newspaper group for its editorial and commercial staff. A predominantly open-plan layout was therefore designed for them by Michael Hopkins & Partners. The *Telegraph* group moved to Canary Wharf in the spring of 1992, prompting the headline 'Fleet Street on the water'.[234]

South Quay Plaza 2, built in 1986–8, is a ten-storey block providing 144,000 sq.ft of office space (*83*), with a shopping mall (opened in January 1989) containing 14 retail units.

South Quay Plaza 3, built in 1988–9, is a 14-storey block providing 210,000 sq.ft of office accommodation. The start-date of this block was advanced because of the speed with which the other phases were disposed of, but ironically it proved difficult to lease or sell, although a restaurant and wine bar on the quayside to the rear of this third block was let in 1990 to Fuller's, the brewers. South Quay Plaza 3 was purchased in 1991 by Wyn-Ro Investments, a joint company formed by Rotch Properties Group (which had previously purchased the shopping parade in the second phase) and the Allied Lyons Pension Fund.[235]

The three main blocks, although of differing heights, are similar in appearance, having reinforced-concrete structural frames and pitched roofs (*49*). Great curtain-walls of black-mirrored glass are set in a grid of blue-powdered aluminium glazing bars, framed by polished black granite, and topped with heavy, Post-Modern pedimented gables, which are echoed by the marble-clad pedimented front entrances, while South Quay Plaza 3 is set on a marble-clad plinth.[236]

Storm Water Pumping Station, Stewart Street 72

In 1969 the GLC decided to construct a new storm water pumping station for the Isle of Dogs on an adjoining site to the old one, built in 1888.[237] These plans did not mature, however, and it was the LDDC, in association with Thames Water, that commissioned the replacement building, which was erected in 1987–8 to the designs of John Outram at a cost of £4 million, including equipment. The main contractors were Peter Birse and the engineers Sir William Halcrow & Partners.

The windowless steel-framed building, designed to be vandal-proof, has the air of a mausoleum and can be best described as Post-Modern Egyptian Monumental, featuring columns, capitals, pediment and overhanging eaves, and having an overall symmetry. It is very colourful, with the capitals of the columns picked out in red, yellow and green and the walls having bands of striped brickwork of yellow, red and purple. The roof is of glazed clay pantiles (*84*).

The overall effect is of a grand, if somewhat unconventional, structure. But the grand architectural features are both decorative and functional: the fat half-columns that rise to the pediment carry the steps and ducts connected with the gantry that runs the length of the turbine hall, and the roundel in the pediment is a gently rotating propeller-like fan which extracts methane gas from the building. Externally, the building echoes and develops themes explored by Outram in the refurbishment of the Harp building at Swanley, Kent, completed in 1987.[238]

The interior is arranged longitudinally into three bays. The pump room, a subterranean chamber 30ft deep, occupies the central bay and houses 14 large pumps that pump water to the large surge tank, housed in the northern bay on ground-floor level, which drains into the Thames. An electricity control room and staff areas on two floors fill the southern bay. Durable materials and bright colours continue inside the building, with exposed facing brickwork, terrazzo floor tiles and brightly painted steel work.

The station was designed to appear half submerged in symbolic recognition of both its function as a 'temple to summer storms' and the machinery hidden beneath it.[239] It stands within a gated walled compound which also contains a smaller transformer building. The new pumping station won a Civic Trust Award in 1989.

The Telehouse Europe (formerly The London Telehouse) 73

This stands in Coriander Avenue, on a 1.4-acre site adjacent to Leamouth Road. It was designed by YRM (Yorke, Rosenberg & Mardall). The project was managed by a Japanese-owned firm, Shimizu (UK), with construction being carried out by John Laing Construction in 1988–90, at a cost of £30 million, for Telehouse International Corporation of Europe, whose shareholders

84. Storm Water Pumping Station, Stewart Street, from the west.

included a number of Japanese interests, as well as British Telecom International. The building, of eight storeys, with a basement car park, is divided into two by a core containing service shafts. Clad in aluminium of varying shades of grey, it stands on stilts, behind a black *brise-soleil* or louvred screen, to protect the inside of the building from direct sunlight. It contains 184,000 sq.ft, including support areas, and provides 24 computer suites, primarily intended as data centres for international finance houses.[240]

75 *Thames Quay, Marsh Wall*

Plans for this office development in three blocks joined by service cores, were drawn up by the architects YRM (Yorke, Rosenberg & Mardall) in 1985 for Fluor Daniel, an American petro-chemical company, who intended to develop the 3.8-acre site as their European headquarters. They required deep-plan office space to accommodate model-makers and design engineers, as well as more standard office space which could be let to conventional users. A decline in oil prices caused Fluor Daniel to aban-

don its plans and in 1987 it sold the site to the National Leasing & Finance Company, which, with Imry Merchant Developers, was responsible for developing the existing scheme. Building work was carried out in 1987–9 by Tarmac Construction, under a £30-million design-and-build contract employing fast-track methods, and still using YRM's design.

The three interconnecting blocks, which are capable of forming a single building, were known as the Lothbury (No. 191), Isis (No. 193), and Wallbrook (No. 195) Buildings, providing accommodation respectively of 71,103 sq.ft, 59,400 sq.ft and 57,738 sq.ft. They are stepped in terraces, which are broken up by escape stairs, bridges, and railings linking different levels (*50*). Each block is U-shaped in plan, with offices arranged around an enclosed light-well. The light-wells run down the front of each block, further dividing up the terraces. To Marsh Wall, there are two pyramidal-roofed single-storey lodges, plus a similar service building. The LDDC transferred its main offices to No. 191 in 1990, while Norex, the insurance, broking and shipping group, moved into No. 195, renaming the building Norex Court.[241]

76 *Tiller Court (Nos 10, 12, 14, and 16 Tiller Road)*

The development originally consisted of four self-contained office units of 9,407 sq.ft, 12,461 sq.ft, 13,038 sq.ft and 13,241 sq.ft, designed by Alan Turner & Associates (project architect David Pearson) for the developer Hastingwood Properties, which itself carried out construction in 1988–90, at a reported cost of £5 million. The five-storey, L-plan block is faced with buff bricks, brown panels (rising to small pediments), and black-tinted glass. Plans for a second phase, to the west of the present building, were put into abeyance and the site has now been utilised for a housing development (see page 44).[242]

79 *Waterside*

This stands close to the south-west corner of the South West India Dock, around Admiral's Way, which runs northwards off Marsh Wall. It was developed jointly by the Wiggins Group, which specialized in motor distribution and house building, and Port of London Properties Ltd, the PLA owning the seven-acre site.[243]

Construction was carried out in the following phases:

1. **Cochrane, Beatty, Scott, Parker, Ladybourne, Drake and Raleigh Houses** (1985–6), designed by Richard Hemingway, consists of 40 small-business apartments in a single quayside block, offset in two parts, and varying from two to four storeys. It is faced in yellow brick and is very domestic in appearance, with hipped roofs and dormers, railed balconies, neo-Classical ground-floor columns, and, to the dockside, enclosed individual gardens or paved areas.[244]

2. **Quay House** (1986–7), designed by Newman Levinson & Partners and erected by John Lelliott, is a three-storey office block of 2,000 sq.m, faced in white concrete, tinted-glass curtain-walling, and painted steelwork, with a pedimented entrance porch. It was taken by British Telecom as a Business Centre.[245]

3. **Ensign House** (completed 1987) is a six-storey office block in hard red and yellow brick, with Post-Modern-style pilasters to the lower storeys, and a hipped, slated roof.[246]

4. **Beaufort Court** (1987–8), designed by Newman Levinson & Partners, is a seven-storey block containing 40 business apartments (totalling 85,000 sq.ft), and five ground-floor retail and showroom units (85). Generally Post-Modern in style, with a central pediment, the building is clad in grey and black polished granite, with glazed curtain-walling, and includes a glazed atrium.[247]

5. **EuroTrade Centre or South Quay Waterside** (1988–92) consists of Dundonald and Waterside Houses, and South Quay Tower. It was designed by the Whittam Cox Ellis Clayton Partnership, and constructed by Wim-

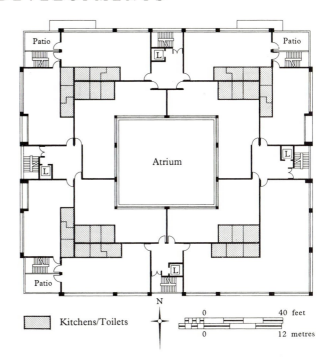

85. Beaufort Court, Waterside, plan of first-floor office suite.

pey, at a cost of £68 million. After the Wiggins Group's shares were suspended in March 1990, a separate company, South Quay Ltd, was formed to complete this part of the development and with the building as its only asset. At the same time, it was decided to divide the block into small business units for sale to investors seeking tax-shelter benefits in the Enterprise Zone, and it was marketed as the EuroTrade Centre. In May 1992 South Quay Ltd was put into receivership and Cork Gully were appointed as administrators.

The U-shaped mainly 19-storey block (also intended to include a shopping mall) has a reinforced-concrete-framed basement but a steel-framed main structure. It is faced in polished speckled-grey granite, and its Post-Modern pediments echo those on the adjacent South Quay Plaza development. South Quay Tower, rising to 24 storeys and a pyramidal roof, looks rather like a smaller version of the Canary Wharf tower (49, 69). Some 350,000 sq.ft of accommodation is provided in 144 self-contained suites, ranging in individual size from 550 sq.ft to 2,000 sq.ft, each with its own kitchen and bathroom. In view of the lack of tenants, the possibility of making these suites into residential units was considered in 1992, but in May 1995 the building was still empty.[248]

6. **The International Hotel, Arrowhead Quay** (1989–92) was designed by Watkins Gray International, and the £28-million construction contract was carried out by Mowlem Management. The 11- and 14-storey block contains 350 bedrooms. The reinforced-concrete structure is clad in granite, with two-storey dark brown anodised curtain-walling infills. After the Wiggins

Group's shares were suspended in March 1990, the unfinished building was sold to Britannia Hotels for £17.75 million, and they completed the development.[249]

7. Site between Arrowhead Quay and Quay House. This remained undeveloped in May 1995, when it was being used as a car park.

80 *West Ferry Printers*

This building, off the east side of Westferry Road, was designed by Watkins Gray Wilkinson Associates (principal architect Ronald Wilkinson), as the *Daily Telegraph* Printing and Publishing Works (*86*).[250] It was built in 1984–6 by Wimpey Construction (UK) Ltd, at an all-inclusive contract price of £30 million, the whole project being costed at about £75 million.[251]

The multi-storey building wraps around three sides of a press hall, and has a steel frame with cast-in-situ concrete floors. It is clad in profiled, colour-coated aluminium, mirror glass and brickwork. The vast press hall, as originally built, was 60m square and 25m high, with its roof supported on massive trussed steel girders.[252]

The fourth side of the press hall was deliberately left open for future development,[253] and a £12.2 million extension, designed by the same architects, was built in 1988–9, with Norwest Holst as the main contractor, for the production of the newspapers of the Express Group, including *The Star*, *Daily Express*, and *Sunday Express*.[254] In May 1995 it was announced that the printing operations of the *Financial Times* were also to be transferred here from their custom-built works in East India Dock Road.[255]

86. West Ferry Printers, Millwall Docks, view from the south-east.

References

ABBREVIATIONS

AJ   *Architects' Journal*
AR   *Architectural Review*
B   *Building*, until 1966 *The Builder*
ELA   *East London Advertiser*
GLC   Greater London Council
GLRO   Greater London Record Office

LBTH   London Borough of Tower Hamlets
LDDC   London Docklands Development Corporation
PLA   Port of London Authority Records, Port of London Authority Collections, Museum in Docklands Project, Museum of London
THLHL   Tower Hamlets Local History Library

CHAPTER I

1. Except where stated otherwise, this chapter is based upon material in Chapters I, X–XIII, XIX and XX of *The Survey of London*, vols xliii, xliv, 1994.
2. A.Yarranton, *England's Improvement by Sea and Land*, pt 2, 1681, p.142.
3. GLRO, MR/UP/46; MR/UP/80A.
4. Museum of London, Museum in Docklands, West India Dock Portfolio, Sheet No.10A; Millwall Dock Portfolio, Sheet No.6: Corporation of London Record Office, Clerk of the Peace, plans 9678A: GLRO, MR/UP/80B-D.
5. Museum of London, Museum in Docklands, Millwall Dock Portfolio, Sheet No.6: GLRO, MR/UP/176,180,184: Parliamentary Papers 1837–8 (661), XVI.9, *Second Report from Select Committee on Metropolis Improvements*, 2 Aug 1838, plan no.31.
6. Guildhall Library, MS 17,205.

CHAPTER II

1. Michael Hebbert, 'One "Planning Disaster" after Another: London Docklands 1970–1992', *London Journal*, vol.17 no.2, 1992, pp.116–17.
2. GLC *Mins*, 1971, pp.248–9: London Docklands Study Team, *Docklands Redevelopment Proposals for East London*, 2 vols, 1973.
3. GLC *Mins*, 1975, pp.285–7,749–51.
4. Docklands Joint Committee, *London Docklands Strategic Plan*, 1976, p.3.
5. *Ibid*, p.81.
6. Peter Hall, *The Cities of Tomorrow*, 1988, p.354.
7. Local Government, Planning and Land Act 1980, Part XVI.
8. Docklands Consultative Committee, *The Docklands Experiment*, 1990, p.7.
9. Ted Hollamby, *Docklands; London's Backyard into Front Yard*, 1990, p.10.
10. LDDC, *Isle of Dogs: A Guide to Design and Development Opportunities*, 1982: David Gosling, 'The Isle of Dogs, London Docklands: Discrepancy in approaches to urban design', *Cities*, Nov 1983, pp.57–158: *Building Design*, 19 June 1987, p.34.
11. *Evening Standard*, 25 June 1990, 'London Docklands 1991' supplement, p.1.
12. Reyner Banham, Paul Barker, Peter Hall and Cedric Price, 'Non-Plan: An Experiment in Freedom', *New Society*, 20 March 1969, pp.435–43.
13. *Building Design*, 15 Feb 1991, p.10.
14. *Independent*, 4 June 1988, p.2.
15. *Building Design*, 6 Sept 1991, pp.8–9.
16. *Ibid*, 14 Nov 1986, p.30.

17. *AJ*, 6 June 1984, p.31.
18. LDDC, *London Docklands Housing Guide*, 1988, p.248.
19. Hollamby, *op.cit.*, p.11.
20. LDDC, *London Docklands Housing Review*, 1988, p.247.
21. GLC *Mins*, 1971, p.248.
22. GLC *Mins*, 1975, p.749.
23. *London Docklands Strategic Plan*, pp.3,14,17.
24. Sue Brownill, *Developing London's Docklands: Another Great Planning Disaster?*, 1990, pp.133–4.
25. *Guardian*, 1 July 1980, p.3.
26. LDDC, *Corporate Plan*, 1986, p.3.
27. *Ibid*.
28. *Ibid*: *Docklands Light Railway News*, No.8, Jan 1989, p.8: *New Civil Engineer*, 4 July 1991, pp.16–21.
29. *Construction News*, 1 Dec 1988, p.8.
30. *B*, 18 Nov 1988, p.7.
31. *Financial Times*, 10 Aug 1989, p.16: *Estates Times*, 23 Nov 1990, p.15.
32. *Economist*, 24 June 1989, pp.35–6.
33. *Construction News*, 22 Sept 1988, pp.16–17.
34. *Independent*, 15 April 1991, p.23.
35. Brownill, *op.cit.*, p.134.
36. LDDC News Release, 29 Nov 1989.
37. *Planner*, 23 June 1989, p.27.
38. Association of London Authorities and The Docklands Consultative Committee, *10 Years of Docklands: How the Cake was Cut*, 1991, p.9.
39. *New Builder*, 31 Jan 1991, p.12: *ELA*, 1 Feb 1991, p.13; 3 May 1991, p.6: *Local Government Chronicle*, 1 Feb 1991, p.10: *Building Design*, 1 Feb 1991, p.3: *Financial Times*, 30 April 1991, p.10: *Docklands News*, May 1991, p.3: *Estates Times*, 3 May 1991: *Independent*, 16 July 1992, p.3.
40. LDDC News Release, 8 Feb 1991: *Guardian*, 4 Feb 1991, p.6: *Docklands Forum*, Feb 1991, p.[4].
41. *The Times*, 16 Oct 1990, p.2.
42. *New Builder*, 2 May 1991, p.5.
43. *New Civil Engineer*, 4 July 1991, pp.16–21.
44. LBTH, *Tower Hamlets Local Trade Developments*, No.17, Nov 1982, p.6: *ELA*, 19 Aug 1983, p.3: *Daily Express*, 23 Sept 1983, p.13: *New Civil Engineer*, 4 July 1991, pp.16–21.
45. *Daily Telegraph*, 24 June 1987, p.21; 6 Oct 1988, p.12.
46. LDDC, *Enterprise Zone Road Improvements*, 1988: *Docklands Recorder*, 6 Oct 1988.
47. *ELA*, 25 Nov 1988, p.14: LDDC, *Keep The Traffic Moving*, 11 Aug 1989, p.[4].
48. LDDC, *Annual Report 1987–88*, p.25: *City Recorder*, 16 June 1988.
49. LBTH, *Tower Hamlets Local Trade Developments*, No.23, Feb 1984, p.5.
50. *ELA*, 30 June 1989, p.21.

51. LDDC News Release, 2 April 1990: LDDC, *Isle of Dogs, Wapping, Limehouse & Poplar Street Plan*, 1988.

52. *Contract Journal*, 12 Oct 1989, pp.14–15: LDDC News Release, 29 Nov 1989: *New Civil Engineer*, 28 March 1991, p.8: *Construction News*, 13 Feb 1992, p.5: *Independent*, 16 Oct 1992, p.8: *The Times*, 17 May 1993, p.31; 18 May 1993, p.8: *Limehouse Link*, 'New Civil Engineer' Supplement, May 1993.

54. LDDC News Release, 8 Nov 1990.

55. *Financial Times*, 11 May 1987, p.34: LDDC News Release, Nov 1989.

56. LDDC News Release, 8 Nov 1990.

57. *New Civil Engineer*, 4 July 1991, p.12.

58. *Stratford Express*, 15 Dec 1967, p.3.

59. *Docklands Redevelopment Proposals for East London*, vol.1, pp.114–15.

60. Light Rail Transit Association, *Transit for Docklands*, c1982, appendix.

61. *London Docklands Strategic Plan*, p.40.

62. Stephen Jolly and Bob Bayman, *Docklands Light Railway: Official Handbook*, 1987, pp.5,32.

63. *Estates Gazette*, 19 April 1986, p.281.

64. *AJ*, 8 Aug 1984, p.23: Information notes issued by the DLR, 17 Sept 1987, p.7.

65. *Guardian*, 29 July 1987, p.4: *Daily Telegraph*, 31 Aug 1987, p.11.

65. Jolly and Bayman, *op.cit.*, pp.13,16,17,47.

66. *Ibid*, pp.22,24,34.

67. *Ibid*, p.40.

68. *AJ*, 8 Aug 1984, pp.22–9.

69. Jolly and Bayman, *op.cit.*, p.10: *Building Design*, 27 Jan 1988, p.36.

70. *AJ*, 8 Aug 1984, p.25.

71. Jolly and Bayman, *op.cit.*, p.12.

72. *Ibid*, p.46: *Guardian*, 8 June 1987, p.20.

73. *Guardian*, 8 June 1987, p.20: *Docklands Light Railway News*, No.9, June 1989, p.1.

74. *Evening Standard*, 18 March 1991, p.50.

75. *The Times*, 23 Aug 1989, p.8; 16 Oct 1990, p.5; 11 April 1992, p.10: *Financial Times*, 15 Nov 1990, p.26: *AJ*, 21 Nov 1990, p.9: *Independent*, 15 April 1991, p.23.

76. *Docklands Light Railway News*, No.9, June 1989, p.1: *The Times*, 23 Aug 1989, p.8.

77. *Independent*, 15 April 1991, p.23.

78. *The Times*, 23 Aug 1989, p.8.

79. Information leaflet issued by the DLR, summer 1990.

80. *Docklands Light Railway News*, No.8, Jan 1989, p.8.

81. *Construction News*, 23 Feb 1989, pp.20–6: Michael Hebbert, 'One "Planning Disaster" after Another: London Docklands 1970–1992', *London Journal*, vol.17, no.2, 1992, p.126.

82. Brownill, *op.cit.*, p.137.

83. Information leaflet issued by the DLR, summer 1990.

84. *Docklands Light Railway News*, No.6, July 1987, p.4: *The Times*, 29 July 1991, p.27: *Evening Standard*, 26 Nov 1991, p.41.

85. *Docklands Recorder*, 17 Aug 1989, p.5.

86. *New Civil Engineer*, 4 July 1991, pp.16–21: *Building Design*, 23 Oct 1992, p.6; 29 Jan 1993, p.5.

87. *Daily Telegraph*, 24 July 1989, p.21: *Financial Times*, 2 Aug 1989, p.6: *Construction News*, 3 Aug 1989, p.52.

88. Information leaflet issued by the DLR, summer 1990: *London Docklands in the News*, No.376, 1 Aug 1990, p.10: *Construction News*, 23 Aug 1990, pp.10–11: *The Times*, 16 Oct 1992, p.23; 17 May 1993, p.33: Information supplied by DLR, 12 Jan 1994.

89. *The Times*, 21 Nov 1990, p.5.

90. *Construction News*, 24 Jan 1991, p.9: *Docklands News*, Dec 1992, p.2: Information from DLR, Oct 1993.

91. *Docklands News*, May 1995, p.3.

92. *Financial Times*, 28 Oct 1991, p.12.

93. *Evening Standard*, 5 Sept 1991, p.5: *Financial Times*, 2 April 1992, p.16.

94. *Docklands News*, Aug 1992, p.9.

95. *Docklands News*, May 1995, p.3: For the most up-to-date account of the DLR, see Alan Pearce, Stephen Jolly and Brian Hardy, *Docklands Light Railway Official Handbook*, 3rd edn, 1994.

96. *London Docklands Strategic Plan*, p.41.

97. Brownill, *op.cit.*, p.144.

98. *Contract Journal*, 30 Nov 1989, p.16.

99. *Guardian*, 1 July 1980, p.3; 7 June 1989, p.13: *Building Design*, 26 May 1989, p.6.

100. *Daily Telegraph*, 24 July 1989, p.8.

101. *Financial Times*, 17 Nov 1989, p.1: *Contract Journal*, 30 Nov 1989, p.16.

102. *The Times*, 29 Oct 1990: *Estates Times*, 3 May 1991, p.1.

103. *Construction News*, 4 July 1991, pp.16–21.

104. *B*, 24 April 1992, pp.18–19.

105. *Independent*, 31 March 1992, p.26; 2 April 1992, p.28.

106. *Evening Standard*, 14 Dec 1992, p.6.

107. *Building Design*, 23 Oct 1992, p.18: *Evening Standard*, 22 Dec 1992, p.4: 22 Feb 1993, p.1; *The Times*, 15 March 1993, p.7; 29 Oct 1993, pp.25,29; 30 Oct 1993, p.7; 1 Dec 1993, p.12: Department of Transport, Press Notice, 8 Dec 1993: *Daily Express*, 9 Dec 1993, p.7.

108. *Docklands Redevelopment Proposals for East London*, vol.1, p.115.

109. LDDC, *Annual Report and Accounts, 1982–83*, p.20: LDDC, *Corporate Plan*, 1986, p.29.

110. *Evening Standard*, 3 May 1988, p.14.

111. *Thames Line PLC*, prospectus, 1987.

112. Leaflets issued by Thames Line during 1988: *Docklands Digest*, No.19, vol.3, 1989, pp.19–22.

113. *City Recorder*, 8 Aug 1991.

114. *Docklands Recorder*, 26 Jan 1989, p.1: *Daily Telegraph*, 2 Feb 1989, p.25.

115. *Daily Telegraph*, 24 Feb 1989, p.2: *Docklands Recorder*, 22 March 1989, p.14: *Independent*, 16 April 1991, p.8: *ELA*, 12 June 1992, p.17; 3 July 1992, p.16: *Evening Standard*, 14 Sept 1992, p.32.

116. *Docklands News*, January 1993, p.3: *Evening Standard*, 19 April 1993, p.54: *Independent*, 21 Aug 1993, p.15.

CHAPTER III

1. *London Docklands Strategic Plan*, pp.18,58–60.

2. LBTH, *Isle of Dogs: a plan for the 1980s*, 1981, pp.23,26–7,29,39.

3. Docklands Consultative Committee/Docklands Forum/Campaign for Homes in Central London, *Priced Out of Town*, 1989, pp.11–12,15.

4. *Ibid*, p.15.

5. *London Architect*, Nov 1981, p.21.

6. *Priced Out of Town*, p.19.

7. *Docklands News*, May 1991, pp.1,3.

8. LDDC, *Annual Report and Accounts*, 1982–3, p.17.

9. See, for example, *London Docklands in the News*, 23 Nov 1984, p.91: THLHL, LBTH Isle of Dogs Standing Neighbourhood Committee, agenda papers, 16 July 1986, item 8.4.

10. THLHL, LBTH Isle of Dogs Standing Neighbourhood Committee, agenda papers, 16 June 1987, item 3.4; 15 Sept 1987, item 3.8; 27 Oct 1987, item 9.10; 21 July 1987, item 15: LDDC, *Annual Review*, 1987–8, p.27: London Docklands Consultative Committee, *The Docklands Experiment*, 1990, p.51.

11. *Docklands News*, Sept 1988, p.16.

12. *Guardian*, 4 Jan 1989, p.22.

13. LDDC, *Housing Strategy Review*, 1989, p.21.

14. LBTH, *Isle of Dogs: a plan for the 1980s*, 1981, p.8 (Fig.1).

15. Sue Brownill, *Developing London's Docklands: Another Great Planning Disaster?*, 1990, p.123.

16. *Docklands News*, March 1983, pp.6–7: LDDC, *Annual Report and Accounts*, 1982–3, p.14.

17. *Priced Out of Town*, p.13.

18. Research Services Ltd for LDDC, *London Docklands Household Survey 1990*, 1991, p.46 & fig.24: LDDC, *LDDC Key Facts & Figures: To 31st March 1994*, p.9.

19. *Guardian*, 3 Nov 1984, p.24.

20. *Priced Out of Town*, pp.19,23–4.

21. *Midweek*, 6 March 1986, p.10.

22. *Priced Out of Town*, p.19.

23. Docklands Consultative Committee, *The Docklands Experiment*,

1990, p.50.

24. *Priced Out of Town*, pp.23–4.

25. LDDC, *Annual Review*, 1987–8, p.26.

26. *Docklands News*, Nov 1989, p.1.

27. *Ibid*, Jan 1986, pp.1,12.

28. *Guardian*, 25 Jan 1986, p.29: *Priced Out of Town*, p.16: *The Docklands Experiment*, p.50.

29. *Guardian*, 25 Jan 1986, p.29: *Financial Times*, 17 July 1986, p.7.

30. Research Services Ltd for LDDC, *London Docklands Household Survey 1990*, 1991, p.25 & fig.5.

31. Association of London Authorities and The Docklands Consultative Committee, *10 Years of Docklands: How the Cake was Cut*, 1991, pp.11–13.

32. *Docklands Digest*, No.32, 1992, p.23; No.33, 1992, p.25: *Evening Standard Magazine*, July 1992, p.115.

33. *Financial Times*, 23 May 1987, p.ix: *Docklands Magazine*, No.6, Oct–Nov 1987, pp.20–1.

34. *Financial Times*, Weekend 9/10 Nov 1991, p.xi: Brian Edwards, *London Docklands: Urban Design in an Age of Deregulation*, 1992, p.7.

35. *B*, 5 Feb 1988, pp.42–7: *Architect, Builder, Contractor and Developer*, Jan 1989, p.32.

36. *B*, 5 Feb 1988, pp.42–7: *Docklands Magazine*, No.23, Sept 1989, p.32.

37. *The Times*, 4 May 1987, p.3.

38. *London Docklands Housing Review*, pp.222–3.

39. *London Architect*, Nov 1981, p.21: *ELA*, 11 Aug 1989, p.6.

40. *Independent*, 10 Sept 1988, p.42.

41. *Financial Times*, 25 Oct 1986, p.xi: *Weekend Guardian*, 26–27 Aug 1989, p.25.

42. *Independent*, 10 Sept 1988, p.42.

43. *AJ*, 8 Nov 1989, p.24.

44. *Ibid*.

45. *Independent*, 10 Sept 1988, p.42.

46. *Priced Out of Town*, p.20.

47. *Ibid*, p.24: *The Docklands Experiment*, p.49.

48. *London Standard*, 11 Sept 1986, p.39: *The Times*, 13 May 1987, p.35: *The Islander*, Nov 1987, p.[1]: *Observer*, 6 Dec 1987, p.58.

49. *Sunday Telegraph*, 1 March 1992, p.xxv.

50. *Financial Times*, 12 Dec 1987, p.x.

51. *The Times*, 18 Nov 1986, p.21: *Financial Times*, 8 Aug 1987, p.viii.

52. *Financial Times*, 12 Dec 1987, p.x.

53. *Sunday Times*, 6 Aug 1989, p.A6a: See also *The Times*, 18 Nov 1986, p.21.

54. THLHL, LBTH Isle of Dogs Standing Neighbourhood Committee, agenda papers, 5 Sept 1986, item 5.2.

55. *Financial Times*, 8 Aug 1987, p.viii; 24 Oct 1987, p.xii.

56. *The Times*, 23 Jan 1988, p.3.

57. *Evening Standard*, 5 Oct 1988, p.29.

58. *Sunday Times*, 6 Aug 1989, p.A6.

59. *Evening Standard*, 5 Oct 1988, p.29.

60. *Guardian*, 10 Sept 1988, p.32.

61. *Sunday Times*, 6 Aug 1989, p.A6.

62. *Independent*, 19 Aug 1989, p.17.

63. *Ibid*, 20 July 1989, p.29: *The Times*, 20 July 1989, p.3: *Daily Telegraph*, 20 July 1989, p.27: *Guardian*, 14 Aug 1989, p.10; 15 Aug 1989, p.2: *Financial Times*, 30 Aug 1989, p.22.

64. *Guardian*, 30 Aug 1989, p.8.

65. *Evening Standard*, 6 Jan 1989, p.7.

66. *Daily Telegraph*, 5 Aug 1988, p.7: *Evening Standard*, 5 Oct 1988, p.29.

67. *Estates Gazette*, 24 March 1990, p.29.

68. *Sunday Times*, 13 May 1990, p.11.

69. *Evening Standard Magazine*, July 1992, pp.107,120.

70. *Building Design*, 22 Sept 1989, p.7.

71. *Daily Telegraph*, 20 July 1989, p.27.

72. *Docklands News*, Aug 1992, p.15.

73. *The Times*, 6 Nov 1991, p.38.

74. *London Docklands Property Guide*, Autumn 1989, p.22.

75. *Evening Standard*, 27 Feb 1991, p.17.

76. *Guardian*, 8 Oct 1990, p.5.

77. *ELA*, 12 April 1991, p.6.

78. *Docklands Forum Newsletter*, Feb 1991, p.[3]: *B*, 22 March 1991, p.17.

79. *Docklands News*, May 1991, pp.1,3.

80. *Building Design*, 22 Sept 1989, p.7: *Guardian*, 8 Oct 1990, p.5.

81. *Independent*, 30 May 1992, p.41.

82. *Daily Express*, 8 March 1991, p.37; 28 June 1991, p.41: *Docklands News*, May 1991, p.6: *Sunday Telegraph*, 1 March 1992, p.xxv: *Independent*, 30 May 1992, p.41.

83. *Independent*, 30 May 1992, p.41: *Evening Standard*, 19 April 1993, p.56.

84. *The Property Guide*, Spring-Summer 1995, p.24.

85. *Ibid*, p.5.

86. *Independent*, 30 May 1992, p.15.

87. *Docklands News*, 9 Sept 1987, p.17: *ELA*, 9 Sept 1988, p.36: *London Docklands Housing Review*, 1988, p.242.

88. *London Docklands Housing Review*, 1988, p.253: *Docklands Magazine*, No.23, Sept 1989, pp.25–34.

89. Information supplied by the LDDC, 12 May 1995.

90. Kentish Homes, sales brochure, 1987.

91. *Financial Times*, 23 May 1987, p.ix.

92. *Landscape Design*, Oct 1986, p.68: *Hackney and Tower Hamlets Chamber of Commerce News and Views*, Spring 1987, pp.19–21: *ELA*, 21 April 1989, p.20.

93. *City Recorder*, 21 May 1987, p.9: *New Civil Engineer*, 24 Sept 1987, pp.22–4: *Construction News*, 21 Jan 1988, pp.22–3: *B*, 5 Feb 1988, pp.42–7: *Docklands News*, Feb 1988, p.10: *AJ*, 24 & 31 Aug 1988, p.13: *New Statesman and Society*, 30 Sept 1988, pp.48–9: *London Docklands Housing Review*, p.225: *AR*, April 1989, pp.28–39: *Building Design*, Supplement, Sept 1989, p.27.

94. *ELA*, 1 June 1984, p.5: *Building Design*, 19 June 1987, p.40: Department of the Environment, *Housing Design Awards, 1987*: *London Docklands Housing Review*, p.227.

95. *Building Design*, 19 June 1987, pp.38–9: *AJ*, 30 Sept 1987, p.65; 17 Aug 1988, pp.20–7: *ELA*, 3 June 1988, p.12: *The Times*, 31 Oct 1988, p.22: *London Docklands Housing Review*, pp.229–30: *Country Life*, 23 Nov 1989, pp.76,78.

96. *B*, 26 June 1987, p.8: *AJ*, 25 May 1988, p.10: *Docklands Magazine*, No.13, Sept 1988, p.24: *Docklands Digest*, No.13, Nov 1988, p.9: *London Docklands Housing Review*, p.232: *Guide to London Docklands*, 1990, p.38.

97. *Docklands Magazine*, Oct 1988, pp.2,4; Oct–Nov 1989, pp.4,6: *London Docklands Housing Review*, p.233: *Architect, Builder, Contractor, and Developer*, Jan 1989, pp.32–3.

98. 'De Bruin Court', publicity leaflet issued by Moram Homes, *c*1988: *Observer*, 8 May 1988, p.50.

99. Information supplied by the LDDC, 16 May 1995.

100. *City of London Post*, 17 Aug 1984, p.6; 12 Oct 1984, p.2: *ELA*, 28 Sept 1984, p.35: *London Docklands Housing Review*, p.234.

101. *ELA*, 21 Jan 1983, p.2: *Docklands News*, Nov 1983, p.5: *London Docklands Housing Review*, p.237.

102. *The Property Guide*, Spring-Summer 1995, pp.10,11: *Docklands News*, May 1995, p.17: Information supplied by the LDDC, 12 May 1995.

103. *Property Monthly Review*, June 1984, p.11: *London Docklands Housing Review*, p.239.

104. Information kindly supplied by Keith Julier of Essex Self-Build Advisory Service, Sept 1990: *ELA*, 15 Feb 1985, p.15: *Docklands News*, Feb 1985, p.5; Feb 1986, p.5; Nov 1987, p.6.

105. *ELA*, 28 Sept 1984, p.35: *London Docklands Housing Review*, p.241: *Docklands Magazine*, No.9, April 1988, p.15.

106. *Building Design*, 19 June 1987, p.43: *London Docklands Housing Review*, p.243: *ELA*, 9 June 1989, p.10: *Docklands Digest*, No.18, [no month] 1989, p.30.

107. Information supplied by the LDDC, 16 May 1995, and by Levitt Bernstein Associates, 5 June 1995.

108. *ELA*, 23 Oct 1987, London Docklands Business Supplement, p.IV: *London Docklands Housing Review*, 1988, p.245: *London Docklands Property Guide*, Summer 1989, p.22: *Estates Gazette*, 13 Jan 1990, p.22.

109. *Daily Telegraph*, 7 Aug 1984, p.15: *Property International*, Dec 1984, pp.100–1: *Building Design*, 19 June 1987, p.43: *London Docklands Housing Review*, pp.247–8.

110. *ELA*, 19 Nov 1985, p.6; 10 May 1985, p.9.
111. Except where otherwise stated, this account is based on *AJ*, 18 Oct 1988, pp.50–6.
112. *Independent*, 7 Nov 1987, p.19.
113. *Daily Telegraph*, 7 Aug 1984, p.15: *Observer*, 6 Dec 1987, p.58.
114. *Independent*, 7 Nov 1987, p.19: *Observer*, 6 Dec 1987, p.58.
115. *Independent*, 7 Nov 1987, p.19.
116. *Ibid: Observer*, 6 Dec 1987, p.58.
117. *The Islander*, Jan 1987, p.[2].
118. *Docklands Magazine*, No.17, Feb 1989, p.47.
119. *The Islander*, Jan 1987, p.[2].
120. *Docklands Magazine*, No.17, Feb 1989, p.47.
121. *ELA*, 6 Jan 1989, p.4: *Planning*, 3 Feb 1989, p.5: *Docklands Digest*, 16 Feb 1989, p.7.
122. *Docklands News*, May 1988, p.4.
123. *The Daily Telegraph Guide to London Docklands*, 1988, p.42.
124. *Observer*, 6 Dec 1987, p.58.
125. *The Islander*, Dec 1984.
126. *Docklands News*, April 1984, p.16.
127. *The Islander*, Dec 1984.
128. *AJ*, 25 March 1987, p.14: *ELA*, 10 April 1987, p.7; 18 Dec 1987, p.10; 22 Jan 1988: *IoD Neighbourhood News*, No.3 [undated], p.2.
129. LDDC News Release, 27 March 1990.
130. *Ibid*.
131. Information supplied by the East London Housing Association and the LDDC, 31 May 1995.
132. Sale particulars from Parris & Quirk of Glengall Bridge, Poplar, *c*April 1988: THLHL, LBTH, Isle of Dogs Standing Neighbourhood Committee, agenda papers, 29 Nov 1988, item 6.2.
133. *The Property Guide*, Spring-Summer 1995, p.10: Information supplied by the LDDC, 2 June 1995.
134. 'Quay West', publicity folder issued by Wimpey Homes, *c*1988: *London Docklands Housing Review*, p.252: *Docklands Magazine*, No.16, Dec-Jan 1988–9, pp.20,23.
135. *The Property Guide*, Spring-Summer 1995, p.37: Information supplied by the LDDC, 16 May 1995.
136. *London Standard*, 11 Sept 1986, p.39: *B*, 19 Sept 1986, p.11: *London Docklands Housing Review*, pp.254–5: *Evening Standard*, 19 April 1993, p.56.
137. Information supplied by the LDDC, 16 May 1995, and the East London Housing Association, 31 May 1995.
138. *ELA*, 23 Oct 1987, London Docklands Business Supplement, p.XI; 22 Jan 1988, p.12: *London Docklands Housing Review*, p.242: 'Island Square', publicity sheet issued by Laing Homes, *c*1989.

CHAPTER IV

1. LBTH, *Achievements in Tower Hamlets Docklands 1976–81*, 1981, pp.5–6.
2. Ted Hollamby, *London's Backyard into Front Yard*, 1990, p.11.
3. *Design*, March 1987, pp.22–3.
4. *Daily Telegraph*, 2 Feb 1987, p.13.
5. *Estates Times Review*, April 1982, p.52.
6. *Financial Times*, 12 Dec 1986, p.6.
7. *Accountancy Age*, 5 Nov 1987, pp.24–5.
8. Hollamby, *op.cit.*, p.11.
9. *Independent*, 15 April 1992, p.17: Brian Edwards, *London Docklands: Urban design in an Age of Deregulation*, 1992, p.137.
10. Edwards, *op.cit.*, p.137.
11. Hall, *op.cit.*, pp.355–7.
12. *Financial Times*, 5 Sept 1985, p.27.
13. *Ibid*.
14. *Estates Gazette*, 13 Dec 1986, pp.1305,1309.
15. *Chartered Surveyor Weekly*, 23 Nov 1989, p.65.
16. *Financial Times*, 5 Sept 1985, p.27.
17. *Economist*, 26 Oct 1985, p.83.
18. *The Times*, 18 Nov 1986, p.19.
19. *Estates Gazette*, 13 Dec 1986, p.1309.
20. *Building Design*, 19 June 1987, p.44.
21. *AJ*, 18 June 1986, p.22.
22. *Independent*, 7 March 1988, pp.8–9.
23. *London Docklands Business News*, Autumn 1992, p.[1].
24. *Docklands News*, Aug 1991, p.8.
25. *Building Design*, 25 June 1993, p.6.
26. *Sunday Telegraph*, 18 April 1993, p.43: *The Times*, 21 April 1993, p.29.
27. *Financial Times*, 12 Dec 1986, p.6.
28. *Docklands News*, Nov 1991, p.13: *The Times*, 14 Sept 1993, p.24; 14 Oct 1993, p.29.
29. *Financial Times*, Weekend, 9–10 Nov 1991, p.XI.
30. *Evening Standard*, 1 Oct 1990, p.17.
31. *Financial Times*, 16 Jan 1988, p.V: *The Lloyd's List*, 15 Oct 1990, p.8: *Money Management*, Dec 1990: *The Times*, 13 Feb 1991, p.32.
32. *Financial Times*, 30 May 1990, p.27.
33. *Chartered Surveyor Weekly*, 17 May 1990, p.11: *Financial Times*, 30 May 1990, p.27.
34. *Daily Telegraph*, 29 March 1988, 'Docklands Development Supplement', p.V: *Daily Express*, 11 Nov 1991, p.41.
35. *ELA*, 15 April 1988, p.4: See also *Daily Telegraph*, 14 March 1989, p.I.
36. *Chartered Surveyor Weekly*, 23 Nov 1989, p.61: *Daily Telegraph*, 14 March 1989, p.I: *Financial Times*, 10 Feb 1990, p.7.
37. *Daily Telegraph*, 29 March 1988, Docklands Development Supplement, p.V.
38. *Financial Times*, 3 Dec 1985, p.8: *The Times*, 27 Feb 1986, p.21; 2 May 1986, p.10; Commercial Property Supplement, 20 May 1992, p.III.
39. *The Times*, Commercial Property Supplement, 20 May 1992, p.III: *Evening Standard*, 8 May 1992, p.13.
40. *Independent*, 23 April 1992, p.23.
41. *Cities*, May 1990, p.121.
42. *Chartered Surveyor Weekly*, 23 Nov 1989, p.61.
43. *Estates Times*, 21 July 1989, p.28: *Daily Telegraph*, 3 Oct 1989, p.xi.
44. *Daily Telegraph*, 3 Oct 1989, p.xi.
45. *Ibid*, 3 April 1990, p.31.
46. *Financial Times*, 8 Nov 1990, p.8.
47. *Chartered Surveyor Weekly*, 17 May 1990, p.11: *Financial Times*, 30 May 1990, p.27.
48. *Daily Telegraph*, 17 March 1990, p.23: *Construction News*, 22 Nov 1990, p.14.
49. *Evening Standard*, 18 Feb 1991, p.50.
50. *Ibid*, 25 March 1991, p.42; 16 March 1992, pp.52–3.
51. *The Times*, 22 June 1991, p.24.
52. *Estates Times*, 3 July 1992.
53. *Daily Telegraph*, 16 April 1991, p.23.
54. *Estates Times*, 15 March 1991, p.7: *Building Design*, 12 April 1991, p.2.
55. *The Times*, Commercial Property Supplement, 20 May 1992, p.IV.
56. *Financial Times*, 30 May 1992, p.6: *AJ*, 20 Jan 1993, p.8.
57. *Independent*, 23 April 1992, p.23.
58. *AJ*, 11 & 18 Dec 1991, pp.56–63.
59. *Evening Standard*, 31 Oct 1992, p.31; 10 Nov 1992, p.54.
60. *Financial Times*, 30 May 1992, p.6.
61. Site location board: *Evening Standard*, 1 May 1995, p.69.
62. *Estates Times*, 26 July 1985, p.4: *B*, 1 Nov 1985, p.33.
63. *London Docklands Housing Review*, 1988, p.246.
64. Information supplied by Whittam Cox Ellis Clayton Partnership, Jan 1991.
65. *ELA*, 4 Feb 1983, p.14; 9 Sept 1983, p.4; 30 Sept 1983, p.3; 12 June 1987, p.3: *The Times*, 15 Sept 1986, p.21.
66. LBTH *Mins*, 1981–2, p.52: *ELA*, 9 Sept 1983, p.4.
67. *Chartered Surveyor Weekly*, 18 Oct 1990, p.17: *Construction News*, 18 Oct 1990, p.10: *Docklands Recorder*, 18 Oct 1990, p.89: *ELA*, 19 Oct 1990, p.16; 27 March 1992, p.12: *Daily Express*, 22 Oct 1990, p.28.
68. *Building Design*, 21 Sept 1984, p.52.
69. *Economist*, 26 Oct 1985, p.83.
70. *Daily Telegraph*, 14 Oct 1985, p.16: *Economist*, 26 Oct 1985, p.83: *Financial Times*, 18 Nov 1985, p.21: *The Times*, 27 Feb 1986, p.21: *Vistas*, Spring 1987, p.22: *Evening Standard*, 25 June 1990, London Docklands 1990 supplement, p.I: *Guardian*, 2 Sept 1991, p.4: 'The Men Who Built Canary Wharf', Channel 4 television

programme, 22 Sept 1991: *Independent on Sunday*, 17 May 1992, p.15.
71. *Economist*, 26 Oct 1985, p.83.
72. *Financial Times*, 18 Nov 1985, p.21: *AJ*, 15 July 1987, p.10: *Docklands Magazine*, No.7, Christmas 1987, p.38.
73. *Guardian*, 26 Nov 1985, p.24: *Art & Design*, Dec 1985, p.9.
74. *Financial Times*, 11 Feb 1986, p.8; 16 Sept 1986, p.6.
75. *Building Design*, 10 Oct 1986, p.3.
76. *Financial Times*, 18 Nov 1985, p.21.
77. 'The Men Who Built Canary Wharf', Channel 4 television programme, 22 Sept 1991.
78. *AJ*, 29 April 1987, p.9; 15 July 1987, p.10.
79. For example, *Financial Times*, 3 Dec 1985, p.8.
80. *Independent*, 16 May 1992, p.17.
81. *Financial Times*, 31 July 1987, p.26: Olympia & York, handout on Canary Wharf, 1 June 1989: *Estates Times*, 15 March 1991, p.7: 'The Men Who Built Canary Wharf', Channel 4 television programme, 22 Sept 1991.
82. *The Times*, 16 May 1992, p.2.
83. *Business*, March 1991: For the background history of the Reichmanns and O & Y, see *Independent on Sunday*, 17 May 1992, pp.14–15, and *Vanity Fair*, Oct 1992, pp.124–52.
84. *Vanity Fair*, Oct 1992, p.129.
85. LDDC Press Release, 17 July 1987.
86. Docklands Consultative Committee, *All That Glitters is not Gold: A Critical Assessment of Canary Wharf*, 1992, pp.19–20.
87. *Docklands Magazine*, No.7, Christmas 1987, p.38.
88. *AJ*, 11 & 18 Dec 1991, p.58.
89. *Canary Wharf: A Landmark in Construction*, 1991, p.40.
90. *Ibid*.
91. Information from Skidmore, Owings & Merrill, Sept 1990.
92. *New Builder*, 20 June 1991, pp.20–2.
93. Olympia & York, *Canary Wharf Fact Book*, Feb 1992, p.6.
94. Olympia & York, *Canary Wharf* (Development Particulars), July 1990, unpaginated: Olympia & York, *Canary Wharf Fact Book*, Feb 1992, p.6.
95. *Canary Wharf*, No.1, March 1988, p.[4].
96. 'The Men Who Built Canary Wharf', Channel 4 television programme, 22 Sept 1991: *The Times*, 16 May 1992, p.2.
97. *Daily Telegraph*, 5 Nov 1987, p.4: *London Docklands in the News*, No.324, 12 July 1989, p.16.
98. *Docklands Magazine*, No.11, Summer 1988, p.38.
99. *Canary Wharf: A Landmark in Construction*, 1991, p.33.
100. *Ibid*, p.24.
101. *Daily Telegraph*, 29 March 1988, Docklands Development supplement, p.V: *Sunday Times Magazine*, 2 Oct 1988, p.17: *Independent*, 5 Sept 1988, p.15: *Sunday Times*, 14 May 1989, p.D14: *London Docklands in the News*, No.324, 12 July 1989, p.16: *Canary Wharf: A Landmark in Construction*, 1991, p.24.
102. *Docklands News*, May 1988.
103. *Estates Gazette*, 12 May 1990, p.22: *City Recorder*, 29 Nov 1990: *Daily Telegraph*, 3 April 1991, p.32: *Sunday Times*, 9 June 1991, p.L3: *Independent*, 13 July 1991, p.27: *Canary Wharf Visitors Guide*, [1991]: Information displayed in Canary Wharf Visitors' Centre, Aug 1991: *Canary Wharf: A Landmark in Construction*, 1991, pp.104–7: *AJ*, 11 & 18 Dec 1991, p.66: Olympia & York, *Canary Wharf Fact Book*, Feb 1993, p.10.
104. *Evening Standard*, 27 Aug 1991, p.2.
105. *Retail Week*, 16 May 1991: *AJ*, 11 & 18 Dec 1991, p.59.
106. Olympia & York, *Canary Wharf Fact Book*, Feb 1992, p.10: *Retail Week*, 6 Dec 1991: *Daily Telegraph*, 25 Aug 1992, p.19.
107. *Sunday Times*, 29 March 1992, p.3.3.
108. *Daily Express*, 14 April 1992, p.41.
109. *Sunday Times*, 19 May 1991, p.4.1.
110. *Financial Times*, 2 May 1991, p.25.
111. *Estates Gazette*, 21 Sept 1991, p.102.
112. *Vanity Fair*, Oct 1992, p.152: *The Times*, 21 April 1992, p.29; 11 May 1992, p.25.
113. *Independent on Sunday*, 17 May 1992, p.15.
114. *The Times*, 11 May 1992, p.17.
115. *Guardian*, 16 May 1992, p.19.
116. *Evening Standard*, 8 May 1992, p.13.
117. *Independent*, 23 March 1992, p.26.
118. *Vanity Fair*, Oct 1992, p.129.
119. *Independent*, 16 May 1992, p.17.
120. *Ibid*, 23 March 1992, p.26.
121. *Daily Express*, 24 March 1992, p.37: *Sunday Times*, 29 March 1992, pp.3.1–3.2.
122. *The Times*, 2 May 1992, p.19.
123. *Ibid*, 8 April 1992, p.21; 14 April 1992, p.17.
124. *Evening Standard*, 8 May 1992, pp.1,12.
125. *The Times*, 16 May 1992, p.17.
126. *Financial Times*, 15 May 1992, p.22.
127. *Independent*, 28 May 1992, p.1: *Evening Standard*, 28 May 1992, p.31.
128. *London Docklands in the News*, 7 Aug 1992, pp.38–40.
129. *Vistas*, Spring 1987, p.22.
130. *Ibid*.
131. *The Times*, 18 May 1992, p.13.
132. *Ibid*, 29 May 1992, p.19.
133. *Independent on Sunday*, 31 May 1992, Business Section, p.1.
134. *The Times*, 30 May 1992, pp.19,21.
135. *Ibid*, 18 June 1992, p.19.
136. *Sunday Express*, 31 May 1992, p.19.
137. *The Islander*, Aug 1992, p.1.
138. *The Times*, 3 June 1992, pp.1,18,19; 6 June 1992, p.19; 13 July 1992, p.17; 14 Aug 1992, p.15.
139. *Daily Express*, 13 Aug 1992, p.41: *The Times*, 13 Aug 1992, p.15; 14 Aug 1992, p.15; 21 Sept 1992, p.23; 25 Sept 1992, p.20: *Vanity Fair*, Oct 1992, p.127.
140. *The Times*, 27 Aug 1992, p.17.
141. *Ibid*, 11 May 1992, p.17; 12 May 1992, p.17; 13 May 1992, p.17; 3 June 1992, pp.1,19.
142. *Evening Standard*, 15 Oct 1992, p.31; 4 Nov 1992, p.18: *The Times*, 12 Oct 1992, p.44; 13 Nov 1992, p.3.
143. *The Times*, 6 June 1992, p.2; 16 July 1992, p.2.
144. *Evening Standard*, 8 June 1992, p.2.
145. *Ibid*, 9 Nov 1992, pp.30–1; 14 Dec 1992, p.6.
146. *Ibid*, 15 Oct 1992, p.35.
147. *Daily Telegraph*, 25 Aug 1992, p.19.
148. *Docklands News*, May 1995, p.3.
149. *The Times*, 3 April 1993, p.21; 20 April 1993, p.1; 21 April 1993, p.29; 23 April 1993, p.26; 6 July 1993, p.24; 26 July 1993, p.2; 29 Oct 1993, pp.25,29; 30 Oct 1993, p.7: *Sunday Telegraph*, 18 April 1993, p.43.
150. *New Civil Engineer*, 15 Oct 1987, p.7: *Construction News*, 12 Nov 1987: *B*, 8 April 1988, p.8: Sue Brownill, *Developing London's Docklands: Another Great Planning Disaster?*, 1990, p.62: LDDC, *Keep The Traffic Moving*, 24 July 1991, p.[2]: Olympia & York *Canary Wharf Fact Book*, Feb 1992, p.24.
151. LDDC, *Annual Review 1987–88*, p.25: LDDC, *Keep The Traffic Moving*, 11 Aug 1989, p.[1]: *ELA*, 6 April 1990, p.6.
152. *AJ*, 6 April 1988, p.8: *Canary Wharf News*, No.6, Feb 1990, p.[3]: *Docklands Recorder*, 6 Dec 1990, p.62: *Chartered Surveyor Weekly*, 6 June 1991: *New Builder*, 20 June 1991, pp.20–2: *Canary Wharf: A Landmark in Construction*, 1991, pp.48–50.
153. *AJ*, 6 April 1988, p.8; 11 & 18 Dec 1991, p.60: *Docklands Magazine*, Summer 1988, No.11, p.38: Developer's Information Sheets, 1 June 1989: *Canary Wharf News*, No.7, April 1990, pp.[2–3]: *New Builder*, 28 March 1991, p.8; 20 June 1991, pp.20–2: *Canary Wharf: A Landmark in Construction*, 1991, pp.54–6: *Independent*, 1 April 1992, p.23: *Docklands News*, Aug 1992, p.6.
154. Olympia & York Canary Wharf Ltd, press releases, 23 March, 22 June 1989: *AJ*, 12 April 1989, p.19: *Building Design*, 21 April 1989, p.1,2: *B*, 21 April 1989, p.22: *Sunday Times*, 14 May 1989, p.D14a: *Construction News*, 22 June 1989, p.3: *New Builder*, 20 June 1991, p.20–2: *Canary Wharf: A Landmark in Construction*, 1991, pp.60–2: *Independent*, 1 April 1992, p.23: *Daily Telegraph*, 25 Aug 1992, p.19.
155. *Canary Wharf News*, No.1, March 1988, p.[4]; No.6, Feb 1990, p.[3]: *AJ*, 6 April 1988, p.8: *B*, 17 Feb 1989, p.12: Developer's handout, 1 June 1989: *New Builder*, 28 March 1991, p.8; 20 June 1991, pp.20–2: *Canary Wharf: A Landmark in Construction*, 1991, pp.66–7: *Morning Advertiser*, 24 May 1991; 19 Sept 1991.

156. *Canary Wharf News*, No.1, March 1988, p.[4]: Developer's handout, 1 June 1989: *New Civil Engineer*, 25 Jan 1990: *New Builder*, 20 June 1991, pp.20–2: *Canary Wharf: A Landmark in Construction*, 1991, pp.67–8.

157. *Construction News*, 8 June 1989, p.12: *B*, 13 July 1990, p.8: *New Builder*, 20 June 1991, pp.20–2: *Canary Wharf: A Landmark in Construction*, 1991, p.72: *The Times*, 12 May 1992, p.17; 15 May 1992, p.17.

158. *AJ*, 6 April 1988, p.8; 11 & 18 Dec 1991, p.60: *Canary Wharf News*, No.1, March 1988, p.[4]; No.9, Dec 1990, p.[1]: *Financial Times*, 29 March 1990, p.1; 8 Nov 1990, p.8: *Guardian*, 9 Nov 1990, p.2: *Docklands News*, Dec 1990, p.3: *New Builder*, 9 March 1990, p.4: *Estates Times*, 13 Sept 1991: *Canary Wharf: A Landmark in Construction*, 1991, pp.19–20: *ELA*, 18 Sept 1992, p.9: *Docklands Recorder*, 19 Nov 1992, p.1.

159. *Daily Telegraph*, 30 March 1988, p.9: *Docklands Digest*, No.21, Vol.3, Dec 1989, p.14: *Canary Wharf News*, No.6, Feb 1990, p.[3]: *ELA*, 30 March 1990, p.15: *Canary Wharf Visitors Guide*, [1991]: *Canary Wharf: A Landmark in Construction*, 1991, pp.76–8: Olympia & York, *Canary Wharf Fact Book*, Feb 1992, p.25.

160. *B*, 15 Dec 1989, p.8: *New Builder*, 13 Dec 1990, p.9: *London Docklands in the News*, No.396, 19 Dec 1990, p.6: *Canary Wharf Visitors Guide*, [1991]: Olympia & York, *Canary Wharf Fact Book*, Feb 1992, p.24: *Daily Telegraph*, 25 Aug 1992, p.19: *Evening Standard*, 22 Feb 1993, p.7.

161. *London Docklands in the News*, No.396, 19 Dec 1990, p.6: *Canary Wharf Visitors Guide*, [1991]: *Daily Telegraph*, 25 Aug 1992, p.19.

162. *Port of London*, vol.LIX, 1984, pp.46–7: *Estates Gazette*, 3 March 1984, p.842: *The Times*, 19 April 1985, p.17.

163. Information supplied by Lawrence & Wrightson.

164. *B*, 19 Sept 1986, p.11: *Independent*, 26 Jan 1987, p.21: *Construction News*, 19 Nov 1987: *Chartered Surveyor Weekly*, 14 Jan 1988, p.39: *Building Design*, 5 Feb 1988, p.48; 22 July 1988, p.3: *City Recorder*, 28 April 1988: *Docklands Magazine*, No.10, May 1988, p.28: *ELA*, 22 July 1988, p.10: LDDC, *London Docklands Property Portfolio*, revised 3 May 1990, pp.6–7.

165. *ELA*, 21 April 1989, p.21; 28 April 1989, p.13: *AJ*, 19 July 1989, pp.42–9: *B*, 1 Dec 1989, p.9.

166. *Estates Times*, 22 July 1988, pp.13–25: *Chartered Surveyor Weekly*, 15 Dec 1988, p.4: *Docklands Recorder*, 16 Feb 1989, p.6: *Financial Times*, 20 Feb 1989, p.22a; 5 Feb 1990, p.12: *Building Design*, 24 Feb 1989, p.16: *Contract Journal*, 31 Aug 1989, p.1: *B*, 22 Sept 1989, p.28; 26 April 1991, Cladding and Curtain Walling supplement, p.11: *Building Today*, 14 Sept 1989, p.5: *Contract Journal*, 31 May 1990: *City of London & Docklands Times*, 14 Aug 1992, p.7: *The London Docklands Guide*, Winter 1992/Spring 1993, p.12.

167. *Estates Times*, 5 Nov 1982, p.2: *Chartered Surveyor Weekly*, 21 July 1983, p.125; 25 April 1985, pp.249–60: *B*, 14 Sept 1984, p.24: *Financial Times*, 2 Nov 1985, p.xii: *Building Design*, 19 June 1987, p.45: Information kindly supplied by Newman Levinson & Partners, 26 April 1991.

168. *Chartered Surveyor Weekly*, 31 Jan 1985, p.244: *B*, 17 May 1985, p.11: *Building Design*, 19 June 1987, p.47: *AJ*, 10 Feb 1988, p.50: Information kindly supplied by Newman Levinson & Partners, 26 April 1991.

169. Unless otherwise cited, the description of this building is based upon the following: *Independent*, 5 July 1989, p.3: *Sunday Times*, 10 Sept 1989, p.38: *New Civil Engineer*, 26 Oct 1989, pp.36–7: *Building Design*, 1 Dec 1989, p.8: *Financial Times*, 22 Jan 1990, p.13: *Docklands News*, Aug 1991, p.12: David Jenkins, *Financial Times Print Works: Nicholas Grimshaw and Partners*, 1991.

170. *B*, 14 Aug 1987, p.9: *AR*, Nov 1988, pp.44,49: Stephanie Williams, *ADT Architecture Guide: Docklands*, 1990, pp.138–9: *New Civil Engineer*, 1 Dec 1988, pp.35–7.

171. *Docklands News*, May 1995, p.6.

172. *Financial Times*, 9 March 1987, p.32: *Glengall Bridge*, publicity booklet issued by Glengall Bridge Ltd, c1987: *Docklands Magazine*, No.5, Sept 1987, pp.38–40; No.6, Oct-Nov 1987, p.46; No.13, Sept 1988, p.28; No.20, May 1989, p.42: *Docklands Recorder*, 20 April 1989, p.7: *Financial Times*, 30 May 1989, p.20: *ELA*, 16 Nov 1990, p.14: *Construction Weekly*, 20 March 1991, p.10: *Glengall Bridge West*, publicity booklet issued by the agents,

Grant & Partners, c1990–1.

173. *B*, 8 Feb 1985, p.13: *Estates Gazette*, 4 July 1987, p.3: *AJ*, 15 July 1987, p.13: *Docklands Magazine*, No.5, Sept [1987], pp.36–7; No.12, Aug 1988, p.34; No.15, Nov-Dec 1988, p.38: *The Times*, 30 May 1990, p.39: *Lloyd's List*, 23 July 1990, p.10: *Building Today*, 26 July 1990, p.5.

174. *Estates Times*, 16 Nov 1984, p.1: *Estates Gazette*, 5 April 1986, p.45: *Building Design*, 19 June 1987, p.44.

175. *Building Design*, 19 June 1987, p.44.

176. Williams, *op.cit.*, p.124.

177. *Building Design*, 19 June 1987, p.44: *Docklands Magazine*, No.10, May 1988, p.28: *Chartered Surveyor Weekly*, 26 Nov 1987, p.14.

178. *Building Design*, 19 June 1987, p.44.

179. *Estates Times*, 18 July 1986, p.3.

180. *B*, 17 March 1989, p.7.

181. *Financial Times*, 5 May 1987, p.29: *Docklands Magazine*, No.10, May 1988, p.28; No.14, Oct 1988, pp.40–1: *Estates Gazette*, 2 July 1988, p.2.

182. *B*, 19 Sept 1986, p.11: *Construction News*, 13 Nov 1986: *Chartered Surveyor Weekly*, 5 Feb 1987, p.8; 10 Nov 1988, offices supplement, p.28–31: *Daily Telegraph*, 11 Oct 1988, p.iii.

183. *B*, 14 April 1989, p.25.

184. *Docklands Magazine*, No.17, Feb 1989, pp.28–9.

185. *Chartered Surveyor Weekly*, 19 Nov 1987, p.10: *Estates Gazette*, 21 Nov 1987, p.995.

186. *Construction News*, 18 Feb 1988, p.12; 21 July 1988, pp.26,47.

187. *Chartered Surveyor Weekly*, 22 Sept 1988, p.7: *Construction News*, 21 July 1988, pp.26,47: *Docklands Magazine*, No.13, Sept 1988, p.28.

188. *Financial Times*, 16 Jan 1988, p.v.

189. *Building Today*, 9 Feb 1989, pp.42,45.

190. *ELA*, 12 May 1989, p.18.

191. *Chartered Surveyor Weekly*, 4 June 1987, p.4: *Construction News*, 21 July 1988, pp.26,47.

192. *Construction News*, 21 July 1988, pp.26,47: *Docklands Digest*, 11 Sept 1988, p.16.

193. *Financial Times*, 30 May 1990, p.6.

194. *Independent*, 24 Sept 1990, p.24.

195. Information kindly supplied by Andrew Dick, April 1991.

196. *Estates Gazette*, 5 April 1986, p.45: *Independent*, 20 July 1987, p.17: *Port of London*, 1987 pt 3, p.98: *Harbour Quay*, publicity brochure issued by the developer, c1987.

197. *AJ*, 23 March 1983, pp.28–31: *AR*, Jan 1984, p.73.

198. *Financial Times*, 9 Feb 1984, p.8: *ELA*, 30 March 1984, p.6; 9 Nov 1990, p.56: *Building Design*, 22 March 1985, p.1; 19 June 1987, p.41: *Chartered Surveyor Weekly*, 26 Nov 1987, p.14: *AJ*, 23 Nov 1988, p.7: Williams, *op.cit.*, p.118: *Docklands Digest*, No.14, Dec 1988, p.14.

199. *Building Design*, 22 March 1985, p.1; 19 June 1987, p.41: *Financial Weekly*, 19–25 April 1985: *Architects' Journal Focus*, July 1988: Williams, *op.cit.*, pp.118–20.

200. *AJ*, 18 June 1986, p.22; 23 Nov 1988, p.7: *Building Design*, 20 June 1986, p.3; 12 Oct 1990, p.1; 6 Sept 1991, pp.8–9: *Estates Gazette*, 3 Oct 1987, p.6; 19 Nov 1988, p.2: *ELA*, 27 Nov 1987, p.21; 19 Feb 1988, p.14: *Architects' Journal Focus*, July 1988: *New Civil Engineer*, 28 Jan 1988, p.10: *Planning*, 23 Nov 1990, p.1: *Daily Telegraph*, 26 Nov 1990, p.18: Edwards, *op.cit.*, p.64: *Docklands News*, June 1992, p.14.

201. Information supplied by Newman Levinson & Partners: *Estates Gazette*, 19 Sept 1987, p.1277: *Docklands Magazine*, No.9, April 1988, p.40: *Contract Journal*, 31 May 1990.

202. *Chartered Surveyor Weekly*, 25 Nov 1982, p.337; 19 Jan 1984, p.151: *B*, 18 Feb 1983, p.66: *AJ*, 15 June 1983, p.49: *Standard*, 16 June 1983, p.9: *Daily Telegraph*, 1 Nov 1983, p.25: *Financial Times*, 4 Nov 1983, Industrial Property Survey: LDDC, *Annual Report & Accounts 1983/4*, inside front cover: *Indescon Court*, publicity brochure issued by the developer, c1984: *British Business*, 4 Jan 1985, p.11: *Industrial Planning and Development*, March 1985: *Docklands Magazine*, No.5, Sept [1987], p.36.

203. *Estates Times*, 31 March 1989, p.3: *AJ*, 5 April 1989, p.12: *Building Design*, Supplement, March 1991, p.II.

204. *Docklands Reporter*, 5 Nov 1987, p.13: *Building Design*, 11 Nov

1988, p.1; 15 March 1991, p.1: *Guardian*, 14 Nov 1988, p.38: *ELA*, 25 Nov 1988, p.14: LDDC News Releases, 11 Sept 1989 and 15 March 1990: *Independent*, 15 April 1992, p.17: *Building*, 15 May 1992, pp.42–6.

205. *B*, 10 Jan 1986, pp.36–41; 27 Feb 1987, p.8; 15 Jan 1988, p.46: *Estates Times*, 23 Sept 1988, p.3.

206. *Chartered Surveyor Weekly*, 25 Nov 1982, p.337; 5 May 1983, p.254; 19 Jan 1984, p.154: 'The Lanterns', brochure issued by the developer, c1983–4: *ELA*, 2 March 1984, p.40; 29 June 1984, p.41: *British Business*, 4 Jan 1985, p.11.

207. LDDC, *London Docklands Property Portfolio*, revised 3 May 1990, pp.3,22.

208. PLA *Mins*, lxviii, p.83.

209. *AJ*, 16 Sept 1981, p.537; 26 Jan 1983, p.25; 9 Nov 1983, pp.32–5: *B*, 3 June 1983, pp.36–8; 13 April 1984, pp.39–46: Academy Editions, *Terry Farrell*, 1984, pp.82–91.

210. *AJ*, 9 Nov 1983, p.35.

211. Academy Editions, *Terry Farrell*, p.85.

212. *Docklands Magazine*, Dec-Jan 1988–9, p.37: *Docklands Recorder*, 22 June 1989, p.9.

213. *Building Design*, 10 May 1985, p.7: *Standard*, 30 May 1985, p.47: *Financial Times*, 17 July 1986, p.7: LDDC, *Annual Review*, 1986–7, p.18: *City of London & Docklands Times*, 26 July 1990: Information kindly supplied by Mr Stanley Trevor, Jan 1991.

214. *ELA*, 10 Aug, 7 Sept, 7 Dec 1984; 7 June 1985; 14 March 1986; *B*, 7 June 1985, p.15.

215. *ELA*, 17 Feb 1989, p.15: *B*, 19 Sept 1986, p.11; 3 March 1989, pp.40–1: *Independent*, 14 Jan 1987, p.5: *Financial Times*, 10 April 1987, p.18: *Construction News*, 16 June 1988: *Leisure Management*, vol.VII, 1988: *The Times*, 8 May 1991, p.21: *The Docklands Guide*, Winter 1994-Spring 1995, pp.15–17.

216. Information supplied by the LDDC, 31 May 1995, and McDonald's Restaurants Ltd, 8 June 1995.

217. *Docklands Recorder*, 27 Oct 1988, p.87: *Docklands Magazine*, No.16, Dec-Jan 1988–9, p.68: LDDC, *London Docklands Property Portfolio*, revised 3 May 1990, pp.3,35: *Building Design*, 8 May 1992, p.3; 24 July 1992, p.32.

218. *Docklands News*, March 1990: *B*, 22 Feb 1991, p.10.

219. *Daily Telegraph*, 2 Dec 1986, p.27: LDDC, *London Docklands Commercial Property Guide*, 1st edn [undated and unpaginated].

220. LDDC, *Annual Report and Accounts*, 1983–4, p.6; 1984–5, p.13: *Port of London*, 1984 pt 2, p.43: *Docklands Recorder*, 26 Oct 1989, p.14.

221. *The Times*, 29 May 1986, p.21c: *Chartered Surveyor Weekly*, 29 May 1986, p.696: *City Recorder*, 20 Nov 1986: *Construction News*, 12 Nov 1987: *ELA*, 27 Nov 1987, p.20: *Docklands Magazine*, No.15, Nov-Dec 1988, p.36; No.19, April 1989, p.34; No.20, May 1989, p.42: 'Meridian Gate', developer's publicity brochure, 1988.

222. *Construction News*, 21 July 1988, pp.26,47: *Docklands Magazine*, No.15, Nov-Dec 1988, p.36; No.20, May 1989, p.42.

223. *Guardian*, 20 Oct 1984, p.16: LDDC, *Annual Report and Accounts*, 1983–4, p.21: *City Recorder*, 2 Feb 1984: *British Business*, 4 Jan 1985, p.11: *Chartered Surveyor Weekly*, 25 April 1985, p.249: *Building Design*, 13 Nov 1987, p.48.

224. *AJ*, 21 Oct 1992, pp.61–6.

225. PLA *Mins*, xli, p.178: *Chartered Surveyor Weekly*, 6 Sept 1984, p.534; 21 June 1990, p.17: *Estates Gazette*, 22 Nov 1986, p.944: *Estates Times*, 9 Jan 1987, p.3; 22 June 1990: *Design*, March 1987, p.22: *Docklands Magazine*, No.9, April 1988, p.42.

226. *ELA*, 13 May 1983, p.5: *Planning*, 20 May 1983, p.16: *The Times*, 11 May 1984, p.18; 12 June 1993, p.20: *Building Design*, 24 May 1985, p.11: Information kindly supplied by Stanley Trevor, Jan 1991.

227. *ELA*, 16 Sept 1983, p.2; 21 Sept 1984, p.9; 26 Oct 1984, p.4: *B*, 23 Sept 1983, p.13.

228. LDDC, *Annual Report and Accounts 1984/85*, p.28: *Estates Gazette*, 19 April 1986, pp.261–83: Williams, *op.cit.*, p.122.

229. *City Recorder*, 25 June 1987: *Port of London*, 1987 pt 3, p.101; 1988 pt 2, pp.64–5: Information supplied by YRM, Feb 1991.

230. *Estates Gazette*, 28 June 1986, p.1412; 11 July 1987, p.142; 16 July 1988, p.3: *Construction News*, 19 Nov 1987: *AJ*, 2 Nov 1988, p.11: *Sweden Today*, Oct-Nov 1988.

231. LDDC, *London Docklands Property Portfolio*, revised 3 May 1990, pp.3,38.

232. *Chartered Surveyor Weekly*, 3 Dec 1987, p.41; 23 Nov 1989, p.39: *AJ*, 20 Sept 1989, p.12: Williams, *op.cit.*, pp.136–8.

233. *Chartered Surveyor Weekly*, 13 Sept 1984, p.615: *ELA*, 27 June 1986, p.35: *Building Design*, 14 Nov 1986, pp.30–1; 11 Nov 1988, p.15: *Docklands Digest*, No.13, Nov 1988, p.15: *Docklands Recorder*, 10 Nov 1988, p.3: 'Skylines 2', undated developer's publicity brochure: Information kindly supplied by Mr Simon Powell of Hutchinson Partners, May 1991.

234. *Estates Gazette*, 31 Aug 1985, p.755: *Financial Times*, 28 Oct 1986, p.8; 30 May 1990, p.27: *The Times*, 18 Nov 1986, p.27, advertisement; 11 May 1992, p.17: *Chartered Surveyor Weekly*, 20 Nov 1986, p.763; 17 May 1990, p.11: *Daily Telegraph*, 1 April 1987, p.2; 27 April 1987, pp.22–4.

235. *Chartered Surveyor Weekly*, 20 Nov 1986, p.763; 17 May 1990, p.11; 8 Nov 1990, p.5; 18 April 1991, p.14: *ELA*, 21 Nov 1986, p.18; 12 Aug 1988, p.6: *City Post*, 8 Oct 1987: *Estates Gazette*, 10 Oct 1987, p.131: *Docklands Magazine*, No.6, Oct-Nov 1987, p.41; No.20, May 1989, p.42. *Docklands Recorder*, 19 Jan 1989, p.1: *Financial Times*, 30 May 1990, p.27: *Property Gazette*, Jan 1991: *Property Monthly*, March/April 1991: *Chartered Surveyor Weekly*, 21 May 1992, p.6.

236. *Financial Times*, 29 Jan 1987, p.30: *Building Design*, 19 June 1987, p.47: *AJ*, 10 Feb 1988, p.48.

237. GLC *Mins*, 1969, p.143.

238. *Brick Bulletin*, Autumn 1987, pp.3–5.

239. *AJ*, 19 Oct 1988, pp.59–63.

240. *Building Today*, 15 Sept 1988, p.5: *London Docklands In the News*, No.285, 5 Oct 1988, p.17: *Docklands Magazine*, No.15, Nov-Dec 1988, p.38: *Contract Journal*, 28 Sept 1989, p.38: *Sunday Correspondent*, 10 June 1990, p.51: Williams, *op.cit.*, p.136: *Building Design*, 15 Feb 1991, p.10.

241. *B*, 18 April 1986, p.8; 11 Dec 1987, p.8: *Financial Times*, 26 Sept 1986, p.11: *Building Design*, 11 Dec 1987, p.4; 13 April 1990, p.10: *Chartered Surveyor Weekly*, 23 Feb 1989, p.13; 15 March 1990, p.4: *Construction News*, 30 Aug 1990, p.32: Williams, *op.cit.*, p.124: S.K.Al Naib, *Discover London Docklands*, 1992, p.58.

242. *Chartered Surveyor Weekly*, 12 Nov 1987, p.9; 26 Jan 1989, p.63: *Building Design*, 27 May 1988, p.15: *Hackney & Tower Hamlets Chamber of Commerce: News & Views*, Summer 1988, p.7: *Docklands Magazine*, No.19, April 1989, p.34: *AJ*, 2 May 1990, p.11.

243. *Financial Times*, 31 July 1987, p.26: *Port of London*, 1987 pt 4, pp.142–3.

244. *ELA*, 12 July 1985, p.7: *AJ*, 27 May 1987, p.84: *Financial Times*, 31 July 1987, p.26: Publicity brochure issued by the agents, Clapshaws, c1987.

245. *Docklands Magazine*, No.1, Winter 1986, p.65: *AJ*, 27 May 1987, p.7: *Building Design*, 19 June 1987, p.45: *Financial Times*, 31 July 1987, p.26: *Port of London*, 1987 pt 4, pp.142–3: Information kindly supplied by Newman Levinson & Partners, 26 April 1991.

246. *Financial Times*, 31 July 1987, p.26.

247. *Port of London*, 1987 pt 4, pp.142–3; 1988 pt 4, p.133; 1989 pt 2, p.29: Information kindly supplied by Newman Levinson & Partners, 26 April 1991.

248. *Contract Journal*, 9 Nov 1989, p.22: *The Times*, 29 Nov 1989, p.7: *Evening Standard*, 30 March 1990, p.14: Information kindly supplied by Mr T. Lundgren of Wimpey, Aug 1990: *Daily Express*, 11 Nov 1991, p.41: *Financial Times*, 16 May 1992, p.11: *Evening Standard*, 31 Oct 1992, p.3; 10 Nov 1992, p.54.

249. *Financial Times*, 3 July 1989, p.12b: *City Recorder*, 27 July 1989: *Daily Telegraph*, 17 March 1990, p.23: *New Builder*, 22 Nov 1990, p.12: *Construction News*, 22 Nov 1990, p.14: *Docklands News*, Aug 1992, p.6.

250. *Daily Telegraph*, 26 July 1983, p.13: *B*, 29 July 1983, p.11; 14 Nov 1986, p.56.

251. *B*, 14 Nov 1986, pp.52,56: *Daily Telegraph*, 27 April 1987, p.22.

252. *B*, 30 May 1986, p.15; 14 Nov 1986, pp.49–56.

253. *Ibid*, 14 Nov 1986, p.52.

254. *Financial Times*, 3 May 1988, p.32: Site information board, Aug 1990: Information kindly supplied by Mr Ray King, Oct 1993.

255. *Docklands News*, May 1995, p.6.

Index

Numbers in italics refer to the illustrations

A000017179423

INDEX